EMPO[WERED]

Autism
Parenting

Celebrating (and Defending)
Your Child's Place in the World

William Stillman

JOSSEY-BASS
A Wiley Imprint
www.josseybass.com

Published by Jossey-Bass
A Wiley Imprint
989 Market Street, San Francisco, CA 94103-1741—www.josseybass.com

The contents of this work are intended to further general scientific research,
understanding, and discussion only and are not intended and should not be relied upon
as recommending or promoting a specific method, diagnosis, or treatment by physicians
for any particular patient. The publisher and the author make no representations or
warranties with respect to the accuracy or completeness of the contents of this work and
specifically disclaim all warranties, including without limitation any implied warranties
of fitness for a particular purpose. In view of ongoing research, equipment modifications,
changes in governmental regulations, and the constant flow of information relating
to the use of medicines, equipment, and devices, the reader is urged to review and
evaluate the information provided in the package insert or instructions for each
medicine, equipment, or device for, among other things, any changes in the instructions
or indication of usage and for added warnings and precautions. Readers should consult
with a specialist where appropriate. The fact that an organization or Web site is referred
to in this work as a citation and/or a potential source of further information does not
mean that the author or the publisher endorses the information the organization or Web
site may provide or recommendations it may make. Further, readers should be aware that
Internet Web sites listed in this work may have changed or disappeared between when
this work was written and when it is read. No warranty may be created or extended by
any promotional statements for this work. Neither the publisher nor the author shall be
liable for any damages arising herefrom.

Jossey-Bass books and products are available through most bookstores. To contact Jossey-
Bass directly call our Customer Care Department within the U.S. at 800-956-7739,
outside the U.S. at 317-572-3986, or fax 317-572-4002.

Jossey-Bass also publishes its books in a variety of electronic formats. Some content that
appears in print may not be available in electronic books.

Library of Congress Cataloging-in-Publication Data

Stillman, William, date.
    Empowered autism parenting : celebrating (and defending) your child's place in the
world / William Stillman.
      p.   cm.
    Includes bibliographical references and index.
    ISBN 978-0-470-47587-4 (pbk.)
      1. Autism in children.   2. Autistic children—Care.   I. Title.
RJ506.A9S757 2009
618.92'89—dc22

                                                      2009009802

Printed in the United States of America
FIRST EDITION
PB Printing   10 9 8 7 6 5 4 3 2 1

CONTENTS

Foreword   v
   Lu Hanessian
Acknowledgments   xv
Introduction   1

PART ONE
Receiving the News   9

1   Could It Be Autism?   11

2   Healing and Acceptance   23

PART TWO
Establishing a Healthy and Supportive
Relationship with Your Child   37

3   Presuming Your Child's Intellect   39

4   Supporting and Interpreting Your Child's
    Communication   55

5   Your Child's Acute Sensitivities   81

PART THREE
Creating Ripple Effects   111

6   Understanding and Using Person-First
    Perspectives   113

7 Autism Advocacy and Self-Advocacy   135

8 Future Pathways   169

Appendix Tools and Resources   177
  Prescription Medication Questionnaire   178
  Pain and Discomfort Inventory   183
  Sensory Sensitivity Inventory   185
  Organization and Specialist Web Sites   186
  Books for Further Reading   191
  Recommended Viewing   195

About the Author   197

Index   201

FOREWORD

When William Stillman first told me he was writing a book on empowering parents of children with autism, I let out an audible yelp of enthusiasm.

"Nobody has written about this, Bill," I said. "And this is the key to what kind of journey parents and their children will either embrace or endure. Whether they will thrive or just survive."

He, of course, knew all that, intuitive guy that he is. So when he asked me to write this foreword, I knew right away that I was called to offer a message to all parents; a message born of more than mere hope or courage or determination. Those are the givens. Parents want to pursue better lives for their kids. They don't typically give up trying to find the right person or treatment or vitamin regimen or approach, model, methodology, or even prayer that can make a positive difference for their precious children.

But when answers are elusive, when stress is pervasive, when cynics and critics abound, when fear and doubt seem to seep into every pore of the parenting experience, many parents unwittingly adopt a kind of quiet resignation, born of fatigue. Born of confusion. Born, ultimately, of outsourcing so much of the journey and responsibility to others whom they perceive to be the true experts on their own children.

We need our learned professionals, to be sure. But when we rely solely on them for advice and trust them implicitly to veto or approve the ways we grow our kids, we walk on dangerously thin ice. This is where we tread fearfully and powerlessly, always worried about the breaking points, the places where we'll be sent into the frigid waters of more chaos and isolation, and where we carry our children on our shoulders.

Every parent makes a pilgrimage. For parents of children with unique needs that pilgrimage requires a unique compass. Parents on this journey willingly take the necessary detours or they ride the brakes.

The pilgrimage is never linear. In the beginning there is anxiety. The despair of *What's wrong with my child?* eventually becomes the outrage of *What's wrong with the world?!* as we grow fiercely protective and defensive of our child's rights to nonjudgmental approaches and to understanding from even the most experienced and revered pediatrician or kindergarten teacher. Along the way our defense turns to curiosity and dogged pursuit—*What do I do now? What can I do?*—as we dare to seek truth. We reach out to others who have gone before, who are on the pilgrimage too—*Whom can I connect with?* And we find kindred spirits. We sew a tapestry and create community—*How can I share my insights?* We feel called. In that calling a newfound courage imbues and drives our every thought and choice, a courage that can come only from our children.

This is what I call having the convictions of our courage. Sometimes, parents don't realize they have convictions—until they find their courage. And they can never fully unearth that courage until they have allowed themselves to be graced by, taught by, and led by the very people who were born with it—their children.

This is when we ask the question, *How can I cultivate my child's innate insights and empower him or her to share his or her light on the world?* This is big-picture parenting.

This is a divine duty.

This is wisdom.

So the pilgrimage, truth be told, is one from chaos to conviction. From fear to love. From doubt to faith. It is a journey to wholeness that can come only from the most splintered of places, a place where nothing made sense and nobody seemed to get it and we doubted our very eyes and ears.

Ten years ago my beautiful, firstborn son came into the world and looked at me as if to say, "Work with me, Ma." Popular opinion was never popular with him. And so I took his cue. I let him navigate while I steered. And he taught me to see. With his delicate sensory sensitivities, afraid of the blender and the lawnmower and the sound of the Velcro diaper tabs coming undone ten times a day, from the beginning he brought me to my senses. Through his own.

"Put him down!" everyone chanted. "You'll spoil him." And I knew that he knew otherwise. So I trusted him.

In the years that ensued, he told me everything he was feeling. "Mom, the world is spinning when I lie down in my bed. I feel like my bed is moving." And it made sense that he wanted a hand on his back to steady him.

"The teacher is like 12,000 pirates trying to steal my lungs, bones, and body," he lamented after the first week of kindergarten. I knew in a flash that he couldn't breathe or move in the classroom. Not in a way that he felt safe. After the principal told me that my son was just "trying to control" me, my husband and I withdrew him from that school, knowing that where there's smoke, there's fire. And so we followed his and our gut.

With uncanny insight, Bill speaks passionately about "presuming intellect." And even in cases where our kids' intellect is obvious because they are highly verbal and gifted thinkers, this presumption holds conspicuously true. Because children who look like they're simply "hyper" or "defiant" or "not listening" or "misbehaving" are more often than not simply trying to cope with the cyclone of discomfort crashing through their bodies.

"He's not listening," said his fourth-grade math teacher. "That's why he doesn't understand what I'm saying." And when I asked her if there was anything I could say to convince her otherwise, she replied, "No."

Misbehavior, as I have often written, is usually "missed" behavior.

And so, as parents, we are faced with a world out there that is more than willing and ready to disempower our children and us—that is, if we succumb to its paradigm, disown our authentic power, and disconnect from our children's needs and truth. There are, as I've learned, ways to bridge the divide. To create mutual understanding. To be proactive, not reactive.

And our children have the key.

"Mom, I feel like I have fifteen radio stations playing in my head at the same time! I wish I could turn off my mind," he has often said.

Our children have information to impart to us. And what we do with that information is the fulcrum. Do we honor it? Ignore it? Dismiss it? Take it like a baton and run with it? Knowledge is power. But knowledge without action is only data.

Knowledge informs. Insight motivates. We derive that insight from our children's clues and cues, from their integrity and our willingness to push aside assumptions and fears and see beyond walls, rules, roles, and unforgiving margins.

Society tends to be symptom-centric, not proactive. As a nation, we often approach our own health and well-being in the same way. But, we don't look deeply into what each symptom might be saying.

Similarly, when we see a behavior, we automatically assume it's the totality of a person. We aren't being deliberately myopic. It's just that we bring all of our stories to the table. We see outwardly as we see inwardly. If we have little empathy and compassion for ourselves, as evidenced by the enormity of our nation's adverse health and staggering, world-leading statistics on depression and anxiety among both adults and children, how can we muster the empathy and compassion for our youngest, most vulnerable citizens?

We must see the person behind the behavior, as Bill has so often said. We need to discover and preserve the parent and the child behind the myths we have created.

And we must shift from misunderstanding to myth understanding.

We must dismantle our mythologies in order to accept the fact that behavior, as Bill points out, truly *is* communication.

Otherwise we cheat ourselves and our kids out of the profound, life-giving opportunity for growth and human connection. It's a dynamic. Even if a child isn't communicating verbally, there is still a dynamic. And to miss that concrete truth is to miss our child's essence, our responsibility to that child and to ourselves, and to our pilgrimage, altogether.

My son has no diagnosis. He never did. No two pediatricians or specialists could ever agree on what to name his "jittery feeling in my chest and legs" or how to explain why he sometimes insisted he couldn't stop moving or giggling or repeating the same phrase or song.

There is no name for his specific and now familiar sensory sensitivities or the way he tends to hear like Swiss cheese when there are too many voices talking to him. Or why he used to miss people's social cues as a preschooler but now deeply understands the subtleties of human relationships in ways that lift the veil for me as a grown person, married for twenty years, and a longtime student of family systems and human dynamics.

"Everyone is born with an amusement park in their heart," he explained to me when he was seven. "And if they don't get the love they need, that amusement park turns into a haunted house. But if people get the love they need, that haunted house can become an amusement park again. It depends how much it shrank."

Eventually, my son's songs became a brilliant penchant for the drums and a gift for making musical instruments. He played in Central Park and gathered a crowd for hours while his jazz filled the air and people gratefully soaked up the offering.

The specialists had once urged us to stop his "perseverative drumming." Imagine if we had heeded their warning. The music would have been silenced. And what would have become of our son's spirit?

Eventually, after much research and gathered insights into physiology, metabolism, and nutrition, his jitters calmed. His self-awareness grew wings, and his confidence soared.

He has grown empowered. I struggled hard to learn it and pass it on, and have often been humbled to be guided back to my own teachings by my son's gentle hand. I am still learning how to be and feel empowered. We are all works in progress.

"I just *know* I'm going to change the world one day," my boy said to me one night in the dark, before bed. "I don't know why, but I feel it deep inside me."

He has reminded me often that he *likes* his sensitive hearing. "It helps me be a better musician," he says.

Empowerment surpasses mere power. It's wrapped in an abiding self-acceptance and self-love. This is the ultimate gift we can give our treasured children—the knowledge that they are accepted and loved for *who* they are. Inside that love is the open sky of possibility.

To be an empowered parent who in turn empowers a child is a steady spiritual rush of purpose and passion that comes only from a pilgrimage that has set its compass and taken its course.

By the time you finish reading this book, you will come away with your compass pointed to the true North Star your child follows, and you may never need to question the validity of your hunches, the legitimacy of your experience, nor the worth of your calling again.

*For Pat, whom
I've long adored*

ACKNOWLEDGMENTS

My great gratitude, as always, to June Clark, literary agent par excellence, and to my editor supreme at Jossey-Bass, Alan Rinzler, whose personal investment in the subject made all the difference in the world. Carol Hartland, Elspeth MacHattie, and Nana Twumasi graciously provided additional editorial support.

Lu Hanessian's foreword is a shining example of proactive parenting possibilities, and I am grateful for the tone she sets, which in turn contributes to the authenticity of my own writing.

Appreciations, too, are due Pat Amos, for her thorough reading of my manuscript, her unconditional support, and her astute commentary. Mollie Boozer, Bill Davis, Mark Freedman, Toni Gage, Laura Manley, Racheal Smith and Phil Killen, Michael Logan, Nick Pentzell, and Wally, Gay, and Wally Jr. Wojtowicz deserve recognition for honoring the autistic experience and for endeavoring that which is right and true and good and kind. Special thanks to Evelyn Sherburne for her touching anecdote about presuming the intellect of her granddaughter. And finally, honors of distinction to Kathleen Dunkelberger for her tireless advocacy against abusive treatment on behalf of her son and all children on the autism spectrum.

EMPOWERED
Autism
Parenting

INTRODUCTION

Recently, a mother's Internet posting caught my attention for its desperate plea. It is one of the thousand-odd postings that are exchanged daily in cyberspace by parents of children with special needs hoping to connect and commiserate with one another or to find someone who understands. Remove the word *autism* from the following transcription and insert Down syndrome, cerebral palsy, dyslexia, or virtually any other so-called childhood anomaly, and the message would still resonate.

> My son was diagnosed a year-and-a-half ago. I have learned that I have to do everything on my own. And I have to fight for everything. But along the way, many professionals have made me feel like they think my son is subhuman. It started with the doctor who diagnosed my son telling me that my son's creativity was only from him coping with me; to some-one saying autistic people don't dream; to other parents not wanting my son to play with theirs once they find out what is really wrong with my son.

> My son is a very sweet and loving little boy whom, if he didn't have this disorder, would be very compassionate. And I also believe he would have a much higher IQ than he does. He is eight with a 60 IQ. It kills me to think that my

son is going to grow up in a world where even some doctors are going to treat him like he was less than a human being. I was just wondering if anyone else out there has felt this way at any time and how you dealt with it, because it's breaking my heart. I wonder if he will even find someone who can see him for the wonderful person he really is.

After the floods, he bought water on his own and took it to the VFW hall and asked them to give it to the hurricane cause. The professionals say he only wanted to do this because my husband and I did a similar thing and he was trying to make us happy. I say my son has a bigger heart than they want to think he does.

This mother's struggle is palpable and conflicted: do her mixed emotions stem from her son's autism diagnosis or do they result from the insensitive affront she's received from the "professionals" in her son's life? At one point, she herself denies his capacity for compassion but a few sentences later cites an act of altruism that confirms the very trait she's been led to believe is absent because of his diagnosis. I could relate, and I'm not even a parent. My way of being, Asperger's Syndrome, or mild autism, dictates that I, too, should lack empathy and concern for others. But if that were true, I probably wouldn't have written this book.

As you may already be aware, autism is one of five clinically defined *pervasive developmental disorders*, collectively considered to be the *autism spectrum*, that also include Asperger's Syndrome, Rett's disorder, childhood disintegrative disorder, and pervasive developmental disorder not otherwise specified.

(You may also hear the pervasive developmental disorders referred to as autism spectrum disorders or ASD.) Each experience has its own unique criteria and yet all share similarities such as challenges in the areas of verbal articulation, social interaction, repetitive actions or vocalizations, physical limitations in movement and dexterity, or absorbing special interests that might get mislabeled as "obsessions."

The intent of this book is not to rehash the kinds of clinical material that you, as a parent, can access at your leisure on the Internet or through other autism literature. *Empowered Autism Parenting* is, instead, just that—not a how-to parenting guide but a volume designed to help you navigate interactions with autism and medical professionals, educators, and the community at large in a manner that will inspire you to serve as your child's voice until he is in a position to advocate for himself.

Much of what is shared here will have application for young people on the autism spectrum with "milder" experiences, such as Asperger's Syndrome; however, this book is perhaps most beneficial for supporting, understanding, and properly interpreting those children with autism who are considered to be significantly impaired but who also have much to teach us that until now has been often unrecognized. When the word *autism* is used it is those individuals to whom I am referring most. (Although autism affects both genders, it occurs more frequently in males and you may note my favoring the pronoun "he" more so than "she" throughout this book, with no disrespect to anyone intended.)

The "celebrating" portion of this book's subtitle implies not only certain human and education rights entitlements but also an awareness of authentic personhood in the form of the gifts and talents your child offers; the "defending" portion pertains to the gross misunderstanding and misinterpretation of autism that has lead to unfair judgments and outrageous acts of verbal and physical abuse, including overmedicating, pathologizing, infantilizing, and marginalizing children so they remain isolated and discriminated against.

It is a curious thing how I've cultivated a reputation as the author of special needs parenting books. At first glance I'm an unlikely candidate because I'm not a doctor, psychologist, or therapist—professionals whose advice has been traditionally sought. But as a self-advocate, someone speaking for himself, I do endeavor to educate others from an *inside-out* perspective, that is, from the perception of the individual with a *different way of being* in order to gain a much-needed and usually overlooked insight.

People often ask me, "When you were a child what was your diagnosis?" and I tell them my diagnosis was *weird*. Weird, moody and irritable, hypersensitive, antisocial, stoic, cold, arrogant and aloof, gifted—those were words that people used to describe me because there was no such thing as Asperger's Syndrome when I was growing up in the 1960s and '70s. There really was, of course, but it, like autism, was considered rare and hardly anyone used it as a clinical diagnosis.

Lacking in agility and coordination (I was the confused kid who unwittingly scored points for the opposing team) but blessed with talent and physical attractiveness, I was without a support system of *any kind* and, because I was a firstborn child, my very young mother and father were probably of the he'll-grow-out-of-it variety—a fact that parents and professionals with whom I speak find inconceivable in today's special needs world of psychologists, therapists, the Individuals with Disabilities Education Act, and Individualized Education Plans.

I was different, unique, peculiar, and standing just slightly off-center, only enough for my experience to be one that I'd grow out of or grow into. My social disconnect manifested not so much in an absence of empathy and concern for others but in an absence of knowledge about *how* to connect in ways that would foster my acceptance. For instance, I clearly recall standing on the recess playground in first grade—watching the other children laugh and run and play—and having *no clue* of what it was that I should be doing and, quite frankly, not especially caring. Nothing about what I observed looked appealing, and this was the pattern that defined most of my social affairs from there on out. I either had no friends or had what others defined as age-inappropriate friendships (meaning I was either friends with children much younger than I *or* I was friends with adults).

As you might speculate, being odd also made me an easy mark. Among my typical peers, I was the object of virtually daily verbal and physical harassment, which eventually yielded to posttraumatic stress disorder and a depression so severe I came inches from taking my own life in adolescence. And yet I endured alone, my parents oblivious and preoccupied with their own agendas—a family equally as vacant of a cohesive emotional connection as was I.

My motivation in compiling this uncommon book is to nurture and inspire wisdom, knowledge, and humanistic understanding in parents of children newly diagnosed with autism, or any different way of being. I want no child to hurt as I once did, and there is really no good reason why any child should.

I am now self-employed as an advocate who speaks out on the value of listening to what others are telling us about their perceived disabilities. Their collective message is usually one of desire for acceptance, "Stop trying to fix me, I'm not broken."

Balancing such respectful listening with effectively parenting the child with autism is an art form that is dynamic and evolves moment by moment. Striking a balance encompasses fair compromise in partnership with your child, unwavering advocacy on his behalf, and the desire to advance a philosophy of compassion and inclusion for all.

I've been working in this field since 1987, but in the past decade there have been dramatic spikes in the numbers of children diagnosed with *special needs*. (The number of children identified with autism has leaped from 1 in 10,000 to 1 in 150.) We've witnessed women's rights, civil rights, gay rights—even animal rights. The next (and arguably the last) great human rights movement is inclusion and respect for persons with different ways of being.

In an era fraught with economic uncertainty, there are no guarantees that *autism services* won't dry up. The financial and emotional tolls oftentimes imposed upon parents of children with autism require revision at once. A period of renewed responsibility has been ushered forth compelling us to become more ingenious, frugal, and resourceful. The time is *now* to initiate a ripple effect that will shatter myths and stereotypes, eradicate intolerance, and foster equality for people with differences—your child included.

And it all starts with *you*, the parent. Surely this is what you wish for your child's future. If so, can you accept the challenge? It won't be easy, and much of what I have to say is radical if not controversial; but it is the truth as I know it to be. And so I'd like to be one resource to you by sharing what I've learned, so that you'll find your own footing along the path.

Here, let me show you the way.

PART ONE

Receiving the News

CHAPTER ONE

Could It Be Autism?

Your toddler or young child isn't developing as you think he should. You're comparing him against your other children, to other kids his own age, what you've read or seen on TV, or what other well-meaning parents (including your own perhaps) are telling you.

Your child is not talking, walking as he should, playing with other children, or playing properly, period. Instead he sometimes seems deaf to your calls, behaves overwhelmed in the middle of Wal-Mart, and lines up Legos by size and color instead of *building* something with them. You've been hearing so much about autism these days—could it be that? The question gnaws at the pit of your parent's gut, the seat of your intuition, and the conflict sets in motion an internal ricochet. Maybe wait a few more months and see; after all, you were a late bloomer. But no, he *should* be toilet trained, enjoying neighborhood birthday parties, and watching *anything* other than the same three Barney videos, over and over, by now.

At the urging of your conscience, you ask your pediatrician: "Could it be autism?" In response you may be coddled condescendingly and made to feel as neurotic as Rosemary in *Rosemary's Baby* for even suggesting anything could be wrong. You may be told that your new-parent anxieties have simply and unnecessarily exaggerated trivial concerns that your child will grow out of in time. In comparison, this scenario may seem like the lesser of two evils—a placating patronization in lieu of the ton of bricks about to drop when you discover the truth: "Yes, your child has *autism.*"

How you react to that word, *autism,* depends on your point of reference and the context in which that word has been communicated to you. Does it conjure despair and desperation? Flashbacks of odd or difficult kids from special ed? Projections of burdensome, perpetual caregiving? In some instances, parents are patted on the head, told to take their child home, and "do the best they can." In worst-case situations, parents are told to institutionalize their son or daughter for life. Now the ton of bricks may feel not unlike a death in the family.

But where is hope? What about love?

Finding Hope

Within the past few years, I've noticed a disturbing trend: parents are telling me their child's autism diagnosis is like "a death sentence" (their phrase). In fact, I've known incidents of parents equating their child's level of functioning with that of a dog! Others have defined their children as "mutants." *Where is this coming from?* In my opinion, it originates from one, or a combination, of two sources.

As an autism consultant, I have had the pleasure of collaborating closely with some terrific, well-informed clinicians who "get" autism as closely as anyone "normal," or *neurotypical*, can; but I have also had the misfortune of interacting with those old-school doctors who cling to their antiquated beliefs about autism (can you imagine that there are *still* mothers being told their inability to bond with their children caused the autism?) and refuse at all costs to confess there may be something new to learn from a different perspective. These are the doctors who are not gentle, sensitive, and compassionate when breaking the diagnosis to parents already overcome with worry.

Instead, autism's supposed pathology—its social and developmental limitations—has been bluntly conveyed, fostering a hopeless prognosis for the future of one's child. Clearly this is not helpful; but given the status to which we elevate our MDs and PhDs, many parents accept this heartbreaking outlook without question, devastated by the loss of the child they envisioned parenting.

Defending this dire prognosis as necessary in order to prepare parents for the worst is without merit, in my opinion. Clinicians are not infallible and none of them can forecast long-term outcomes and capabilities accurately for *any* child with autism. My friend, fellow author, and self-advocate, Stephen Shore, had been recommended as a candidate for institutionalization as a youngster—he now has his doctorate and travels the world advising on autism issues. As I once told a couple lamenting their child's diagnosis upon returning home from the doctor's office, the child in the backseat of their car is still the *same* child he was on the trip to the doctor; the only thing that's changed is their perception of him based solely on a label, a single word: autism.

Additionally, the mass media are responsible for dividing our humanity into two camps: us and them. Personally, I am wearied and angered by news reports I hear or read that define those on the autism spectrum as "afflicted sufferers stricken by a devastating disorder that robs them of their ability to function normally." If you are the parent of a child newly diagnosed by one of the aforementioned clinicians (of the not-helpful variety), having that doctor's bleak and hurtful prognosis reinforced by the media's tragic spin on autism can be devastating! There have been several recent incidents of parents actually murdering their child with autism. I can't help but wonder if consuming guilt and unrealistic pressure hasn't driven these parents to believe that a world without their child in it is the better alternative.

The curious thing is we *all* have autism to one degree or another! We've all experienced neurological crossed wires that result in motor-control blips, misfires, and disconnects.

Know Your Own Autisms

Ever awaken in the middle of the night and realize your arm is "asleep" from the elbow down? It is a common situation experienced by nearly everyone at one time or another. As much as your brain is willing that arm to budge, it's deadened to the signals or impulses your brain is sending it—a neurological impotence, if you will. How many of you have actually had to physically move the asleep arm with your other hand in order to free up circulation and regain its use?

If that same paralysis harbored in more than one limb, or your voice box, you might experience autistic-like symptoms, or something akin to autism's possible "cousins," such as Asperger's Syndrome, dyslexia, Tourette's, Parkinson's, Alzheimer's, cerebral palsy, ALS or Lou Gehrig's disease, ADD, ADHD, OCD, sensory integration disorder, and a realm of other human experiences on the neurological continuum.

You have experienced additional autisms if you've

- Driven from Point A to Point B, but upon arriving at Point B you have no recollection of the drive.

- Begun driving from Point A with Point B as your final destination but intending to make a special stop to pick up something or someone—and you end up driving your regular route, having forgotten to make the detour.

- Been driving along, hear a song you like, and you intend to listen all the way through, but soon realize your mind has wandered and you haven't heard a word of it.

- Been driving along and you hear a song you haven't heard since high school—and what happens? Experiencing the song immediately conjures memories of that era in your life. We create strong associative connections in the same way with scents and smells (of food, cologne or perfume, or tobacco) that we link in memory to certain people and places, as well as to life-defining events such as an accident, a birth or death, or a disaster of some sort (you could probably relate details about where you were and what you were doing on September 11, 2001).

- Happened upon someone familiar while out shopping, but seeing her out of the context in which you know her somehow prevents you from recollecting her name on the spot (although it may come to you after you've had sufficient process time).

- Had to retrace your steps physically in order to remember something, or thought you'd misplaced something (a pair of scissors or your eyeglasses, perhaps) and then suddenly realized you'd been holding it the whole time you were searching for it.

- Lost track of time or self-awareness (no need to eat or use the bathroom) while immersed in an activity for which you hold great passion (painting, dancing, gardening, watching a film, or the like).

- Had a case of the giggles so severe that you could not regain your composure until the experience ran its course.

- Been so angry, or afraid, that words escaped you in the moment.

- Absolutely *had* to scratch an itch, and could not focus on anything else until you were so relieved.

- Been so overcome with worry and anxiety that you couldn't sleep, or were restless, tossing and turning all night.

- Calmed your anxiety by biting your nails, tapping a pen, shaking your leg, rocking yourself, twirling strands of your hair or toying with a piece of jewelry, or talking or humming to yourself.

- Created a new pain, by biting your lip or chewing the inside of your cheek, for instance, in order to take your attention away from a stronger, involuntary pain.

- Experienced uncontrollable shivers so intensely that your teeth chattered involuntarily.

- Struggled to decipher the meaning of certain words in the appropriate context, such as in the sentence, "she shed a tear over the tear in her new dress."

- Had to ask someone to slow down or repeat the name or phone number you're trying to transcribe.

- Been unable to hear the TV reporter because you were focusing on reading the news ticker at the bottom of the screen.

- Organized your items in your kitchen cupboards, bathroom, work space, or clothes closet in alphabetical order (canned goods with labels facing out), by color coordination, or at right angles.

- Come in from frigid weather and found your hands so numb with cold you could not use them to hold an eating utensil, write longhand, or unbutton your coat.

- Had a song in your head that absolutely would not go *away!* It may have been *The Star-Spangled Banner,* a commercial jingle, or a Barry Manilow tune. You may even have awakened in the middle of the night hearing the song you cannot seem to banish. Imagine how it would feel if that experience of being stuck with the song in your head (which precludes your thought processes) transferred throughout your body, or lodged in your throat and hindered your vocalizations?

These common experiences—*brain fades* or instances in which the *body vetoes brain signals*—affect us all, making us kindred in our humanity. But if you did them with any degree of regularity, *you'd be eligible for an autism diagnosis!* The next time someone suggests your child's hand flapping or finger flicking is maladaptive, gently remind them that they do it too; it looks just like the times they sit and shake a leg or tap a pen!

Seeing Beyond the Backroom Kids

From the outset, as you've read, many parents are given a grim projection for their child's future. They are led to believe their child with autism is incapable, unaware, and of substandard intellect, a lost cause that will always function at the level of a four-year-old, even as an adult. This often results in parenting approaches of two extremes: either tireless endeavors to eradicate autism through high-cost, intensive, one-on-one (adult to child) behavioral therapy for countless hours on end (which in some cases may also involve a regimen of physical restraints and antipsychotic medications), or an abdication of effort that results in *backroom kids,* children with autism who are left to their own devices with little supervision or interaction.

The proper response to autism is to reenvision this diagnosis as a neurological disconnect that can be related to the disconnects of cerebral palsy, Tourette's, Hodgkin's, Parkinson's, recovering from a stroke, or any other such experience that compromises brain-body connections and impairs movement or articulation of speech. Even though many aspects of the physical body are unreliable or not of good service, the *cerebral* aspect is intact, thought processes operate at capacity, and mental capability is completely competent (it just doesn't measure that way through IQ scores). It's important for parents to know that there is emerging scientific research to support the reevaluation of people with autism, using nonverbal intelligence testing to reveal their true intellect commensurate with, or beyond, their chronological age.

Some parents who don't foresee true intellect as a possibility for their children, have bought into the myth of autism—that autism equals intellectual inferiority or mental retardation. In addition to shame and guilt, despair, denial, and hopelessness may prevail. These parents begin thinking only of day-to-day maintenance and minimal standards of caregiving. Hence they tend to create their own backroom kids.

I see these children, watching me from their baby-gated existence within the screened-in porch or the distant bedroom at the rear of the house. Many of them don't have much meaningful connection with their families. They have free rein to do as they please because their parents are afraid to apply fair discipline or have been told not to bother because their child won't understand.

Some backroom kids are overweight, have poor diets, and are provided age-inappropriate books, toys, and videos. Some are still on bottles and in Pampers at age five . . . six . . . *nine*. This is unacceptable.

When I meet them, I think: "I see you there, little one. You with your grubby bag of orange cheese curls and the *Veggie Tales* video looping repetitively. You with your bright, glistening, welcoming eyes. You with your hunger for knowledge and information beyond the backroom, or even your backyard. I see how very smart you are inside. I see *you*."

Deconstructing the Myth of Autism

Refusing the myth of autism, building relationships founded upon a belief in competence, and challenging autistic intellect is what will create a cultural shift for the growing numbers of very young children diagnosed with autism each day. It will also yield hope for the adults with autism who have endured in silence, offered only Little Golden Books, Strawberry Shortcake puzzles, and *Lady and the Tramp* videos.

The regrettable irony is that we have a long and unfortunate history of backroom kids—*retarded defectives* as they were once known—only in earlier eras the backroom was often confinement to the basement or an attic with a door locked from the outside. Shame and guilt were very much a motivation for those parents then, as much as they are for some parents now.

Isn't it curious that what's called for is simply adjusting *our* behavior to our own true interests, and compelling ourselves to be more sensitive—to listen more carefully with our eyes and hearts as well as with our ears? We're not only talking about presuming intellect, we're talking about demonstrating a renewed respect. As much as we all (including some "experts" in the medical community) are on a learning curve about autism, we are also all on a curve of similarities and differences in our collective human experience. This begs the question, Is there really any such thing as *normal*?

Maybe autism isn't really as *autistic* as it seems. Let's consider that your child with autism presents an opportunity to the world, to command and compel acceptance and compassion for diversity in the same ways that the rights of others— African Americans, Latinos, Asians, Native Americans, and members of the gay community—have been championed.

Rest assured, given the proper respect, appreciation, and opportunity your child with autism *will* change the world in ways that are right and true and good and kind.

CHAPTER TWO

Healing and Acceptance

Since your child's autism diagnosis, have you found yourself in "why me?" mode? If so, you may be feeling a longing for resolve, understanding, and support. Do not allow the pessimistic perceptions of others to place limitations on your child's potential. Do not allow ignorance to color your parent's intuition about your child's true intellect. Consider the significant stress level of marriages in families with a child with autism and that it's also commonplace for moms of such kids to be depressed. Instead of asking "why me?" take stock of your resources.

Do you have a supportive spouse or partner? Do you have family and friends upon whom you can rely? Have you accepted previous challenges in your life successfully? Do you have the tools, the terminology, and the proper perspective to benefit you and your child? This book is intended to aid you in developing the latter, but are you aware of the variety of formal and informal resources accessible by you?

Many parents contend that simply being able to connect and commiserate with another parent in similar circumstances helps immeasurably. The community pages of your telephone book may guide you to no- or low-cost services offering counseling, early intervention, child care, and financial assistance; but you may also learn of parent support groups, meeting groups, and other local autism organizations through your county human services agency. Additionally, if you have Internet access, you may find it convenient to communicate with other parents (worldwide) through any number of online Web sites, blogs, message boards, and listservs, many of which are referenced in the Appendix at the back of this book. Parent to Parent USA (www.P2PUSA .org) may be a good place to start if you are feeling alone in your journey and wish to connect with other moms and dads in your state and even in your hometown.

If you are someone who turns to your faith in difficult times, you may be interested to know that studies have shown that families' commitment to their spirituality or religious practices can directly affect their ability to coalesce and to overcome obstacles as a family unit. Those families who are devout in their faith have been shown to cope with their child's autism with reduced stress and solid conviction.

Perhaps this is one difference between parents who see the glass half full and parents who feel doomed by autism. That is not to suggest that anyone should conclude that the absence of religious beliefs is a predictor of deficient parenting, bad attitudes about one's child, and feeling unable to rise to meet the challenge. But this finding does, perhaps, point to the importance of a core of resilience and resolve.

Why *Not* Me?

One mom who was feeling sorry for herself described her "why me?" mentality as being in "victim mode" until she realized "why *not* me?" She came to feel she was destined to parent her son because of her humanitarian skills, her ability to advocate loud and clear, and her strength in navigating service systems. Indeed, these traits have served her well in raising her son.

Would you be surprised to learn that I hear from a number of parents who are informed by their children with autism that they were *chosen* as parents by their child, prior to birth and with deliberate intent? (In one instance, a mom told me her son said he chose her over a Japanese couple because he didn't want to learn their complex language!)

The autistic experience comes with many challenges that we must surmount in order to lovingly support our children and to assimilate their acute sensory sensitivities into a world that is oftentimes overwhelming and intolerant of diversity. But autism also comes with myriad gifts if you can be open to seeing this perspective. Your child *requires* you in her life; and, indeed, dozens of parents have told me they are better—even more spiritual—people than they would've been had they not been blessed to raise a child with autism.

Perceiving your child's way of being in the context of the big picture of life lessons and unconditional love may aid you in putting your circumstances into proper perspective. Allow yourself time to mourn, should need be, but if you persist in feeling *punished* for a prolonged period of time, it may be very helpful to consult with someone from a local place of worship or a community counselor in order to sort through the issues and formulate a plan to move forward with optimism.

Toni Gage has two children on the autism spectrum and a husband with Asperger's. She shares her newly altered perceptions about her boys in these words:

> My children are so wonderful and are growing into the most fascinating young men. I tell them everyday how important they are and how much they are loved just the way they are. I have to stress it to them when they come home from school and have been drilled about how they are supposed to behave. I know they have to live in a society where they are constantly judged but I do see change in the world.

Optimism is essential to your child's well-being and self-perception, and this begins with the tone *you* set. But that doesn't mean you have to go it alone. Essential to your capacity to advocate for your child is your surrounding yourself with a support team made up of people who "get it," that is, family, friends, relatives, and those autism professionals who understand your child in the gracious manner that you do and who are poised to agree with some or all of the philosophies put forth in this book.

As you become more knowledgeable and savvy about autism as it pertains to your child's individual experience, the support team may be expanded to include day-care providers, babysitters, educators, neighbors, and others with whom you and your child have relationships. People who accept your child without exceptions will be invaluable to a support team ready to defend your child's place in the world. Such a team will also provide you with additional sustenance, confidence, and resilience to speak up and speak out on your child's behalf.

Do Labels Matter?

Your child may not only be diagnosed as autistic, she may also be labeled with additional distinctions such as "severe autism" or low- or high-functioning autism. This type of diagnostic judgment call only further serves to perpetuate parental fear and anxiety by setting you up for the worst of expectations because of your child's *perceived* limitations. I have even seen parents express great relief in the presence of other families that their child is high-functioning, and I've heard others dismiss their child as incapacitated, restricted by the label, for being low functioning. I've actually been introduced to children by parents who say, "Meet William; he's severely autistic."

Our society has long held the irreverent belief that people should be labeled and compartmentalized in order to identify their differences, or even their so-called pathology. For the labelers, setting an "us" and "them" precedent allows those who self-identify as "us" to feel superior while keeping "them" at arm's length by refusing to acknowledge the kinship of everyone's mutual humanity. For the person being labeled, the action also establishes a precedent: that of feeling a sense of inequality, of feeling degenerate, and of feeling hopeless.

I should know, having felt this way myself growing up; and I've received countless messages through my Web site from adolescents and young adults with autism who are depressed and suicidal, having grown up believing all the deficit-based labels put upon them. The damage created by "us" and "them" labels is plainly evident (more about this later).

How important are labels to *you?* One parent I know was influenced by another family member to accept a label of both autism and ADHD (attention deficit/hyperactivity disorder). I could tell by her description of her daughter that she loves and adores her daughter unconditionally. She was also well aware that her daughter experiences a different way of being that requires a mother's sensitivity in making compassionate accommodations as her daughter integrates with the world at large.

I could appreciate her wanting to know how best to support and educate her child as early on in life as possible, and as in her circumstances, this knowledge usually occurs through the attribution of a label. I imagine that the labels of autism and ADHD have gained this mom and her daughter access to certain services and supports as well. So, for the time being, the labels may be useful (as names only), but the labels are an *incomplete truth* about the whole child that is her daughter.

Knowledge is power, and—labels aside—your ability to know and understand how your child with autism thinks and learns and processes information will be your most invaluable tool as her loving parent and strongest ally.

No Pity Permitted

The unfortunate truth is that not everyone will love and adore your child as you do. Those not understanding of his acute sensitivities may reject him, call him lazy, incapable, subhuman, or retarded. This sounds harsh, but I'm preparing you now for the worst.

You may also find yourself the charitable recipient of pity, sympathy, and even glorification for parenting one of "those" children. You may be told you're a saint or an angel. You may find yourself being told, "I'll pray for you," *because of* your child's autism. This reaction may come as a form of dismissal due to the speaker's discomfort, or it may be fear driven.

Accept no pity, and rest assured that no matter what, your child with autism is designed precisely as he is intended to be—naturally and perfectly. Your child is entitled to his place in the world, and he has great gifts to offer—the same as *any* child.

Legitimate prayer is driven by love and compassion and a desire to be of service. The next time someone says, "I'll pray for you," suggest that she pray not for your child but that a greater sensitivity may flourish in us all, leading to an acknowledgment of our kindred humanity.

What those who wish to set themselves apart (or above) others with different ways of being fail to recognize is that—at the current rate of occurrence of autism revealed in the statistics—it is *they* who could soon be in the minority, if they're not first rendered disabled by virtue of an accidental calamity, a genetic predisposition to bad health, aging, or unsuitable health and lifestyle choices. Any one of us could find ourselves with an autistic-like manner as the result of a serious accident or stroke. If this happened, we would still wish others to remain steadfast in the belief that we are competent despite our physical transformation, wouldn't we? We'd want others to allow us the process time to respond to a question without second-guessing our needs if we were unable to recall, say, an associate's name instantaneously, and we would want to be permitted the chance to enjoin our impervious limbs, to move without having a caregiver hastily "doing it for us" because it's time efficient. We wouldn't require pity; we'd require *compassion*.

Ask Not What Causes Autism, but What Autism Causes

What causes autism is the subject of an increasingly heated nationwide debate that is not likely to subside any time soon. Most prominent among the multiple theories is that too many childhood vaccinations in quick succession—and the toxins therein—induce rapid regressions in children developing typically. Previously it was thought that the mercury preservative, thimerosal, in the mumps, measles, and rubella vaccine was the culprit, but it was eliminated from the vaccine over a decade ago. Many books and journals have continued to focus on the vaccination theory, and some individuals in the public eye have crusaded to have the public accept their point of view.

This vaccination theory does, though, beg a number of questions. If the vaccines overwhelm the physiology of very young children, does this event induce autism or does it accelerate emergence of autistic symptoms already present? Is the experience of those children who become violently ill after receiving certain vaccines (and who appear autistic-like) the same thing as autism? And what of those children unaffected by vaccinations who are later diagnosed with autism?

Other theories about what causes autism include the idea of a genetic strand that naturally predisposes some children to the autism spectrum. There may be truth in this theory because, through my work, I've come to speculate that some undiagnosed adults are the parents of the children with whom I'm consulting. Yet another notion is that exposure of a fetus to external environmental toxins in utero (toxins inhaled or consumed by its mother) may be a cause, as may be what is said to be a more accurate diagnosis of autism in individuals who would have been labeled with intellectual deficiency in another era.

Other theories range from the plausible and worthy of research to the downright outlandish, such as middle-aged fathers, indifferent mothers, mothers who are depressed or who have extended ring fingers, too much television, too much cell phone use, a mixing of different ethnic groups (!), even extra-terrestrials (!!)—well, you get the picture. We're purveying paranoia that envisions an "epidemic invasion" of sorts.

As a result, many Americans are being panicked into believing that virtually *anything*—the theory du jour—is culpable for causing autism. Not only that, Americans may be lulled into thinking that autism is a phenomenon isolated to the United States. It's not. It is occurring worldwide. It is estimated that there are approximately 1.5 million people with autism here, but the number in China is comparable. Our statistics indicate 1 in 150 children have autism, but in Ireland it's 1 in 110, and in the United Kingdom it's 1 in 100. Autism shows no signs of abating despite research and studies and awareness and fundraising. I have seen a projected date—2035—for the time when most *everyone* will have autism of some sort or another! And at this rate, concurrent with research efforts, it's high time we began to focus on not just what causes autism but *what autism causes*.

Positive Transformations

Thank goodness we human beings are different now from what we were as Neanderthals. We've made innumerable, extraordinary advances. It's called *evolution*. But what's to say we're going to remain as static as we are at present? What's to suggest that we won't evolve further still and emerge as different from our present selves as we now are from cavemen—and what precisely would that look like if it were to occur?

A radical proposal about the true value and benefit of autism's impact on the evolution of human beings might be to suggest that there's a purpose for autism being in the world; a renaissance, a rebirth, and a call to reverence for all of humanity. This is not to suggest that we should patronize people with autism in some glorified extreme, but they do have many special and valuable qualities that would be good for everyone to emulate. They tend to have less need for words, they desire to live in peace and quiet, and most of them don't comprehend aggression or competition as necessities. I hear regularly from parents of children with autism who, as a result of understanding and caring for their child, have been compelled to *slow down* and really focus upon what's important in life—not the highest-paid position, the fastest car, the biggest house, or the most expensive wardrobe but love and compassion for their child with a unique and different way of being.

One mom told me that autism made her finally "grow up" and become a responsible adult. In appreciating the role of being her son's foremost advocate, this mother rose to the occasion and accepted the challenge, emerging as someone who, in her own eyes, is braver, optimistic, and better organized than she otherwise would have been. Other people have told me that they've undergone dramatic transformation. For instance, Bill, father to son Christopher, said, "I was a violent, angry man until I met my son. Thank God for autism and the changes it has brought about: human beings without prejudice, spiritual beings full of love—what a fantastic epidemic."

Of course not everyone is in a position to attain such surrender and sacrifice. It may be argued that disagreement and dissension will keep rising in accordance with autism's statistics. But be advised that the numbers of children diagnosed with autism will also continue to grow, silently and surely and without any singular explanation. Instead of creating further divisions of opinions, we should collectively endeavor a compromise that balances research for causation with the *inside-out* perspectives shared in this book.

Your Child Is Not a Science Project

When I was young, I used to watch Mutual of Omaha's *Wild Kingdom* every Sunday night. I don't know that it particularly intrigued me, although I did have a strong interest in animals and nature at the time. What anguished me, though, was that I could never understand why the camera crew didn't *intervene* and rush to the aid of the random wildebeest savaged by a leopard! I didn't comprehend that they were allowing nature to take its course by not interfering. In some ways, this may be an apt metaphor for the way in which autism should be perceived by researchers and the medical community.

You may occasionally hear about—or be offered the opportunity to participate in—various tests, trials, or experiments for children with autism, advertised by your local hospital or university. These opportunities may range from sleep studies to nutrition reviews to medical procedures. Some may profess to be beneficial to your child or family, which may hold especial appeal, and I'm aware of families that sign up for such studies as often as they are offered.

But wait!—who's giving consent? Has anyone asked the *child* what he thinks, or whether he agrees it may hold some benefit? One autism study in particular required at least a two-week commitment for the child to *live* on-site in an artificial environment.

Let's think about this for a moment; think about your child. Does it make sense to uproot him from everything familiar, everything that helps him to feel safe and comfortable and in control, in order to subject him to an experiment conducted by strangers, in an unfamiliar and strange environment, and without his permission? And don't you think the researchers may be more likely to get precisely the "autistic behaviors" they're seeking simply because the child is in such an environment?

Of further concern, some studies desire to test the effects of certain medications on children with autism; these are called *investigational medication* trials. Turn on the television at any time of day or night for no more than fifteen minutes, and you will notice that every other commercial is for a medication. It seems there's a medication for every human ailment: anxiety, depression, aging, erectile dysfunction, obesity, sleeplessness, and overeating, so it's only logical that there are those who believe autism can be managed and controlled with pills.

This mind-set may even extend to your child's pediatrician who desires to prescribe medication to treat "autistic behaviors." But the world of pharmaceuticals is very much an industry. And in June 2008, an exposé reported that Harvard medical doctors received over $2 million in consulting fees, much of which was unreported, from pharmaceutical companies that manufactured antipsychotic drugs (that is, major tranquilizers) that the doctors had endorsed for use in treating children even though long-term drug efficacy in children has not been properly established. Whom are we really trying to benefit by promoting drugs instead of exploring alternatives? (Even still, many parents are unable to name their child's medication, prescribed to control "autistic behavior," and others are unaware of the potential side effects or even the *desired* effect of the medication.)

Let's be clear: *you don't medicate autism*. You don't medicate a *natural* experience any more than you'd dispense pills to someone born blind, with Down syndrome, or with cerebral palsy. So if your child is taking prescription medication for sleep, "behaviors," obsessive-compulsive disorder, or just plain autism, please refer to the medication questionnaire found at the back of this book. It should aid you in fully understanding the impact medication may be holding for your child.

Be cautious, sensitive, and respectful of your child prior to entertaining the notion of allowing your child to participate under experimental circumstances in treatment in which "autism professionals" wish to interfere with his or her course of nature—which, like *Wild Kingdom*, may in fact involve a camera crew.

In one situation, for which I was consulted, Sarah, four years old, was considered nonverbal but was spontaneously speaking with her support staff with whom she shared mutually pleasing interactions. However, she was not speaking with her own family. Her mother spent her four weeks of annual time off from work taking Sarah to various doctors and autism-related appointments where Sarah was poked, prodded, and otherwise examined. Sarah was also openly and unfavorably compared against her twin. Not only did she not have a *reason* to talk within her own family, she also began—at just four years old—manifesting symptoms of depression that could be traced to feeling as though there was something terribly wrong that any number of doctors couldn't seem to fix.

Please don't misunderstand me—I'm not suggesting that we do *nothing*. But *how* we do what we do is what makes all the difference. And it is what we do within the context of a respectful, reciprocal *relationship* that matters most of all. The next section of this book may affirm your parenting and provide key revelations as you explore positive approaches to a healthy and supportive relationship with your child.

PART TWO

Establishing a Healthy and Supportive Relationship with Your Child

CHAPTER THREE

Presuming Your Child's Intellect

"IM NOT RETARDED IM SMART NOT A MENTAL GIANT BUT I AM INTELLGENT."

These are the words that were communicated to me by a sixteen-year-old young man whose rural high school classroom I visited on a crisp and wintry January morning. Like most teens his age, he took classes in keyboarding and computers, and was a fluent two-handed typist. But his classroom was anything but typical; it was for kids in special ed, and my new friend was autistic and virtually mute, a man of very few words. And yet the words he conveyed upon our first meeting formed a declaration that belied his physical appearance and asked me to presume an intellect intact.

It was a credo I had heard and *read* from countless others before him; from children and adults who felt the need to qualify their unconventional mannerisms, vocalizations, and assorted neurological blips, disconnects, and misfires by imploring, in essence, "Don't trust your eyes. This isn't really all there is to me. See past my deceiving exterior, see beyond my label." And indeed, I always assure them that I see clearly their gorgeous humanity and profound potential.

The desire to simply be welcomed and accepted is universal to all human beings, but there are those among us who struggle in the endeavor for worthiness—who struggle to be considered whole and complete and competent.

Even though I've enjoyed a career as someone who intuitively connects to those on the autism spectrum, I have long known that this concept of presuming intellect was not important exclusively to people with autism. Upon becoming conscious of it, I realized that an assumption of incompetence in those with different ways of being surrounds us with glaring reality throughout each day. It shows in the way most people publicly avoid the brightly beaming man with Down syndrome; in the adult son who berates his elderly mother compromised by confusion; in the impatience with which people tune out the person who stutters; in the small child everyone thinks wants to be tickled, swung through the air, and have her hair tousled, but who actually has a strong aversion to being touched; and in the individual who is blind yet truly capable of ordering her own meal but who nevertheless hears the server deferring to her companions, "And what will *she* have?"

Refusing this typical standard, a friend of mine, Evelyn, instead went so far as to presume the intellect of her infant granddaughter. She shares the surprising outcome of this idea through the following anecdote:

> As a school psychologist, and as a parent, I have always appreciated the way knowledge gained in one role enhanced the skills in the other role. In the last year I have become both a student of children on the spectrum and a two-day-a-week caregiver to my first grandchild. Although I am constantly

cautioning support staff that not all strategies that work with neurotypical children are effective with children with autism, it seems to me that all of the sensory interventions I am learning work with all children.

I remember in my own early childhood years many experiences where intellect was not presumed and where adults talked about me, rather than with me. In my work with small children, I frequently see parents and caregivers either label behaviors in blaming generalities: "he's cranky," "tired," "demanding" . . . or take them personally: "he hates his dad," "he's angry since I went to work," rather than seeing behavior as the only viable form of communication in pre-verbal children.

I had an opportunity to try out my newfound skills in an interaction with my granddaughter. She usually takes a nap by falling asleep on my shoulder after letting me know that she is tired by rubbing her eyes. On this day, she looked at my shoulder and started alternately bucking her head into my chest and pushing me away. Instead of personalizing: "she misses her mother," "she hates me," or blaming: "she's entering the terrible twos early," "she's overly tired" . . . I decided that she was communicating to me that I had overloaded one of her senses. I looked down at my bright orange ribbed sweater and decided that either the color or texture were not soothing and conducive to falling asleep. I covered my shoulder with a cloth diaper, patted it and said "soft." She looked at the diaper, at my face, back at the diaper and then laid her head down and went to sleep.

A Belief in Competence

In late 2007, a national advertising campaign was launched in connection with New York University's Child Study

Center in order to raise awareness about childhood disabilities, including autism and Asperger's Syndrome, among others. Although the motive was altruistic, the campaign's fatal misstep was the manner in which it sought to raise awareness through a series of hostage notes—images of threats scrawled on notepaper as written to parents "from" their child's disability. Here is the content of those ads that sought to address the autism spectrum:

> We have your son. We will make sure he will not be able to care for himself or interact socially as long as he lives. This is only the beginning.
>
> Autism

> We have your son. We are destroying his ability for social interaction and driving him into a life of complete isolation. It's up to you now.
>
> Asperger's Syndrome

But what the campaign's devisers failed to realize was that their shock-and-awe tactics for attention also riled the ire of self-advocates (persons with autism), parents, and professionals deeply offended by the advertising's assumptions of defectiveness and incapability. After a swift, nationwide backlash led by autism self-advocates, the ad campaign was dismantled and discarded—and an important lesson about respect and a belief in competence was (one hopes) advanced.

I have written about and discussed the concept of presuming intellect for many years, but I am still struggling to communicate this intention well enough for people to put the concept into practice. For example, I was prompted to clarify this contention in greater detail after I learned that an autism professional led a video crew into a family's home for the purpose of taping their child's "autistic behaviors." Although the parents gave permission for this, no one thought to ask or even inform the child, so that when the video cadre showed up very early one Saturday morning, they not only surprised and disrupted the child's routine, *they got precisely what they came for*—the child protested their presence loud and clear, and rightly so!

Traditional intelligence quotient examinations have been unsuccessful at tabulating the true intellectual capacity of individuals with autism, and emerging research from clinicians Meredyth Goldberg Edelson and Morton Ann Gernsbacher, among others, is disproving the common notion that autism is equable with mental retardation. On the contrary, presuming intellect is the prerequisite to establishing a respectful, reciprocal relationship with your child.

Ten Essential Points for Celebrating (and Defending) Your Child

The following ten points are essential for developing your advocacy skills so that you are able to celebrate and defend your child's place in the world until he is in a place to advocate for himself. Presuming intellect requires that we appreciate the following:

- *Don't define people by their diagnosis.* Remember playing tag? Nobody wanted to be *it*. And if you were *it*, you wanted to get rid of *it* because being *it* was stigmatizing, a detriment, and something undesirable—that was the game; being *it* was to be avoided and feared. Remain *it* longer than we'd like and we are challenged to catch up to the others, to belong, and to feel accepted. When we define someone by his diagnosis, our perception of him may become something to be dreaded: he's someone defective, someone who has the *it* with which we don't wish to risk an association of any sort. For the person so perceived, this attitude is the lubricant that greases the wheel for the vicious cycle of a self-fulfilling prophecy. That is, when people define you as having *it* and that's all you know of yourself, you will reflect back precisely what others project upon you. This is a natural and defensive reaction; and if you don't speak or can't articulate your feelings, your outpourings of "behaviors" will only further validate the diagnosis (hence the vicious cycle).

- *Shatter myths and stereotypes.* Clinical diagnosis is but a framework for explaining behaviors or atypical attributes. A diagnosis may include judgments about severe intellectual and physical limitations and further speculation about other incapacities. However, it wasn't so long ago that persons who were epileptic, homosexual, or even left-handed were labeled as mentally deviant. This led to unfair, inaccurate, and unjust myths and stereotypes.

  All of psychology and psychiatry is educated *guesswork*; no single clinician can state with absolute authority what someone experiences in the way that medical specialties usually can. In considering three factors, insight, foresight, and hindsight, we need to encourage others and ourselves to look beyond humankind's history of deficit-based labeling in favor of perceiving a person's humanity—regardless of her diagnosis or way of being. The label, which may perpetuate clinical myths and stereotypes, is an incomplete truth; it should be but one point of reference in fully supporting the whole person.

- *Don't talk about people in front of them.* Have you ever been in conversation with two or more people and someone talks out of turn, interrupting, belittling, or disputing your contributions? Or have you temporarily lost the use of your voice as others tried to interpret your wants and needs? How did either instance make you feel? If we don't value what people have to offer, especially if they are unable to speak, we send a message of superiority versus inferiority. When we define people by their diagnosis and perpetuate myths and stereotypes, we presume the authority to talk about them in front of them as an entitlement. After all, it shouldn't matter if we share information about someone's behaviors with his parents, doctors, and others in front of him because he is retarded, autistic, and unaware—right? Wrong!

Presuming intellect requires us to believe an individual's intellectual competence is intact. This means we do not speak about him in front of him in ways that are hurtful, embarrassing, or humiliating. It also means that we employ *person-first language* ("boy *with* autism," not "*autistic* boy"), because that compels us to be conscious of the words we use when discussing someone.

- *Interpret "behavior" as communication.* Have you ever been so angered that words escaped you in the moment, and the only way you could express yourself was by screaming or throwing something? You probably felt justified in your actions because it was the only way you could vent your expression of extreme upset. But what would life be like if you could *never* retrieve the words you wanted when you needed them and if you *always* seemed to be grappling with overwhelming or frustrating circumstances that caused you to react in extreme ways as the only option? In the same way that you could rationalize your own behavior, let's remember that we *all* have good reasons for doing what we're doing, and we're doing the best we know how to do in the moment.

  You may respectfully deconstruct behavior in terms of *communication* by appreciating the following three reasons why people may engage in what others call "acting out" or "aggressive behaviors": (1) The inability to communicate in ways that are effective, reliable, and universally understandable. (2) The inability to communicate one's own physical pain and discomfort in ways that are effective, reliable, and universally understandable. (3) And the inability to communicate one's own mental health experience in ways that are effective, reliable, and universally understandable.

- *Offer communication enhancements and options.* We have become a culture that values instantaneous, rapid-fire responses to our need for information. Consider the immediacy with which we now communicate with one another through e-mail, instant messaging, and text messaging and our round-the-clock accessibility via cell phones. When others do not communicate with us on a par with the manner to which we've become accustomed, we may lose patience, become bored or distracted, or dismiss their communication attempts altogether. This may be especially true when we communicate with those challenged in articulating language, such as small children, the elderly, and those with a neurological difference resulting from stroke, Tourette's, Alzheimer's, cerebral palsy, or autism. We may wrongly interpret the inability of others to speak as quickly as we'd like as an incapacity, when in fact it's a matter of our sensitively allowing a process time beyond what is standard for those individuals to find the right words or retrieve spoken language.

In providing support to others, we must acknowledge that not everyone is neurologically "wired" for verbal communication; this is *not* the same as not having something to say. It is unacceptable to accept that because someone doesn't speak, there's nothing we can or should do. There are myriad communication options and opportunities to offer as speech alternatives. We can make use of pointing to "yes" and "no," some basic sign language, photographs and symbols, computers and other keyboards, and technology of all kinds. The individual can guide us to the device, or combination of devices, that makes sense for her. Ultimately, engaging in conversation by discussing someone's most passionate interests in the context of a mutually pleasing relationship is a great incentive to entice someone into trying a communication alternative that is new and different.

- *Offer age-appropriate life opportunities.* When we are insensitive or disrespectful of an individual's intellect, we have a belief that the individual likely possesses a juvenile aptitude, childish thought processes, and skills on a par with someone who is chronologically much younger. This stereotype of the perpetual child may lead us to interact with the stigmatized individual in ways that are pretentious, patronizing, and insulting. It also means that we limit the life opportunities that we offer individuals, in favor of preserving the perpetual child mind-set. Instead of *age-appropriate* opportunities, we provide adolescents, adults, and even persons who are elderly, with dolls and toys and with reading and viewing material suited and intended for very young children.

  You can only know what you know; and if someone is only ever afforded such limited opportunities, a child-like affect persists and permeates our interactions with him. *But,* if we presume intellect and acknowledge that an individual's behaviors might really be cries of boredom or offense with educational curricula, vocational options, or recreational activities that are dehumanizing, we will know better how to partner with him in planning age-appropriate learning, work, and free-time opportunities. The greatest obstacle to implementing this is our own attitude and how we perceive supporting someone with a different way of being.

- *Make compassionate accommodations.* Have you ever been trying to read or listen attentively to something when someone near you is constantly coughing? You can react in one of two ways: either with annoyance or with consideration. Reacting with annoyance will only foster bad feelings in both parties; you may feel as if the person should know to be more socially considerate, and the person, who may be struggling to care for herself, may feel hurt or attacked. Reacting with consideration may include approaching the individual gently to offer her a cup of water, a mint, or a lozenge or to simply commiserate with her about a human experience we've *all* endured at one time or another. Responding with the latter approach requires discounting initial impressions and making a compassionate accommodation, not only in our thoughts but in our deeds.

In considering compassionate accommodations for the individual with a different way of being, think in terms of *prevention* instead of *intervention*. *Prevention* means knowing fully what an individual requires *in advance of* a situation, environment, or activity in order to feel safe and comfortable and able to partici-pate. This relates to the ability to think, communicate, motor-plan movement, and assimilate with the senses. It means foregoing the antiquated model of multiple, overwhelming community integrations (which often sets the overloaded individual up for an *intervention*) in favor of simple, subtle, and interest-based activities in a qualitative relationship context. For example, your child may desire to collaborate with you to create a kitchen recipe but may have a strong aversion to crowds. Instead of shopping for the recipe items as part of your weekly shopping during peak grocery-shopping times, plan to shop with your child for those recipe items only and to do it first thing in the morning, when the store is virtually empty, to ensure a successful activity.

- *Respect personal space and touch.* If we perceive someone in our care to be less than equal, be it a child, adult, or someone elderly, we seem to feel entitled to touch his physical being in order to meet our own needs. For example, instead of allowing someone the time required to bathe, eat, or dress for himself, we may grow impatient and begin handling him ourselves to "get the job done." Or, in desiring to be affirmed, we may initiate physical touch by embracing, back rubbing, or hair tousling—all of which may be intrusive, unwelcomed, and without permission. (In recent years, some colleges have recognized a version of this problem and have implemented *touch protocols* for dating co-eds, to avoid misinterpretation of touching as sexual aggression.) Conversely, many of us are extremely uncomfortable brushing against other people in the cramped quarters of an airplane, bus, subway, or train.

  Personal space and touch are a matter of individualized perception for each of us, based upon our culture, upbringing, and relationship experiences. A friendly slap on the back, which you've been conditioned to convey as a way of communicating "hello," may send shock waves through the nervous system of the recipient. Instead, respectfully await the invitation *in*. Await the acknowledgment that coming closer, touching, even making eye contact, is welcomed. The invitation *in* may be as subtle as someone who rarely makes eye contact locking eyes with you and tracking your movement, or an individual carefully, gently, extending a finger to initiate touching you. Be very mindful of the mixed messages we send to children whom we routinely embrace and then confuse once we define such touching as "inappropriate" when they reach adolescence. It is also fair to state your own acceptable preferences for touch limitations.

- *Seek viable employment for others.* The human services system that serves people with different ways of being endeavors to be altruistic and well intentioned, but it is an industry nonetheless; one that in seeking viable employment opportunities for its clients, attempts to conjoin with mainstream industries that may be unpresuming of intellect. More often than not, this translates to menial tasks that are believed to require no thought: repetitive factory work, janitorial cleaning up, emptying trash receptacles, or replenishing the fast-food salad bar, to name a few. For most people, such jobs are temporary stepping-stones; but for persons who are perceived as largely incapable, these employments have become a norm that perpetuates stereotypes.

  In seeking to pursue viable employment for our children when they are eligible, we need to think in terms of cultivating gifts, strengths, and talent areas as early on in their lives as possible. Begin by identifying an individual's most passionate of interests—those subjects or topics that she wants most to talk about, watch, draw or write about, reenact, engage with, and read about. Such interests may include astronomy, Greek mythology, traffic signals, dinosaurs, ocean mammals, and specific movie characters with whom your child identifies. When we value passions instead of labeling them as obsessions (unless they seriously impair a person's quality of life), we are better poised to envision a creative blueprint of possibilities for the future. These may include higher education, virtual employment via the Internet, or self-employment opportunities.

- *Acknowledge that we are all more alike than different.* Remember the last time you drove somewhere and, upon arriving, had no recollection of the drive? How about when you hear a song you haven't heard since high school, and memories you associate exclusively with that era come flooding back? Or what about the times you've halted, blocked, stuttered, or stammered over calling up someone's name? These are examples of common neurological blips, misfires, and disconnects that make us all kindred in our humanity. While others may have traits that appear more exaggerated, like physically rocking or hand flapping, you may catch yourself engaging in a similar action if you've been shaking your leg, tapping a pen, or twirling your hair or a piece of jewelry.

When we embrace the philosophy of presuming intellect we are in a position to become agents of transformation. Doing so requires forgiveness of our own ignorance—which need not hold negative connotations—as well as seeking the forgiveness of others whom we have not held in the same regard as our typical peers. This means approaching your child privately, gently, and respectfully to offer an apology for talking about him in front of him or for not fully presuming his intellect. Wouldn't you do the same for *anyone* with whom you have a valued relationship? You may just be surprised by the forgiveness you receive from your child for being so genuine and sincere.

We have become a culture that elevates perfectionism to exalted heights, which is an unrealistic and potentially damaging aspiration. When we acknowledge the kinship we share with one another, we are most apt to value diversity in our lives within the context of mutual respect, collaboration for the greater good, and the presumption of intellect.

A relationship with your child began in utero and was affirmed the first time you gazed upon him, held, and nuzzled him. But, in looking back, did you find yourself daunted and disheartened if your child with autism cried at your touch or pulled away sharply—seemingly acts of rejection? The preceding ten tenets will aid you, and those you seek to influence, by providing a humanistic framework from which to reenvision the manner in which your relationship may be mutual, reciprocal, and respectful.

One mom told me that after learning about the philosophy of presuming intellect, she went home and apologized to her five-year-old son with autism for not recognizing how deeply affected he had been by a traumatizing experience. He not only embraced her in great relief, for the first time ever he said the words, "I love you."

CHAPTER FOUR

Supporting and Interpreting Your Child's Communication

Many people on the autism spectrum are unable to communicate verbally in ways that are effective, reliable, and universally understandable. *Effective* means it works; *reliable* means it works when I need it, and *universally understandable* means it works with everyone, wherever I go.

It is reported that at least 50 percent of individuals diagnosed with traditional autism don't talk, and still others don't talk in ways others can readily discern. Instead, these individuals have had to find other ways to communicate and get their needs met, like pointing to something or pulling us to what they want. This is, of course, very limiting, and you may be conscious of this if you've struggled to understand what your child is trying to tell you by verbalizing, gesturing, or guiding you—but you keep getting it wrong. The frustrated outpourings of these miscommunications only increase as the child ages and expands his range of wants and needs, and can lead to the point of self-injury such as head banging or biting and scratching one's own flesh.

The next time you are with a group of coworkers, friends, or family, think what life would be like if you all were sealed off from the rest of the world and all use of your voices was forcibly removed. Your little colony also has absolutely no access to computers or even menial pen and paper. How would you communicate? Through eye contact and facial expressions, or through gestures or primitive sign language? What if the sum of your communications was reduced to a relentless rendition of charades? You might be able to get the most essential of your needs met—eat, drink, bath-room, sleep—but gesticulations and furtive gazes are open to individual interpretation. And they can't possibly capture everything that you'd be thinking, envisioning, imagining, hoping, and dreaming. Imagine the hellish frustration of that existence, being of full intellectual capacity but having no clear way to communicate it.

Now let's revisit persons with autism in this very con-text. We want and expect more in the way of communica-tion than eat, drink, bathroom, sleep; but this is so often how children with autism live each day—just meeting basic needs. Let's first appreciate the strength and resilience that each individual possesses in getting those needs met *every day*, often without communication that is effective, reliable, and universally understandable. This alone elevates the mastery of survival tactics and coping mechanisms to an art form.

Mollie is a professional with whom I have consulted on a number of situations. With her master's degree in social work, she is someone who was taught and trained to believe in behavioral treatments, and she relates, here, her appreciation of the autistic charades so imperative to understanding her seven-year-old client, Emily.

> I have learned one very important lesson: behaviors *are* a form of communication! I started consulting with Bill Stillman because of changes in Emily's behaviors. She would scream, cry, stomp her feet, throw herself on the floor, and at times would push or forcefully throw herself on the support staff person. Through the course of the monthly consults, Bill would suggest to me that Emily was desperately trying to communicate to me and others that something was wrong! Among other things, such as sensory sensitivities, Bill would recommend that I investigate Emily's home life and the people that are in it. In an attempt to find out what she was trying to communicate, I started to talk with her mom about changes occurring at home.

> At the time, Emily's mom had a new boyfriend and the family was in the process of moving. I had attributed all of these changes to her behaviors, but several months went by, and no positive changes in Emily's behaviors were seen. In talking with a friend of the family (with mom's permission), we discovered that recently the boyfriend had begun drinking often and was verbally abusive toward Emily's mother. Emily couldn't tell me what was wrong, but, looking back, all of the signs were there and I am sorry that I missed them. The signs were so obvious too. She, at times, cried and would refuse to get on the van to go home at the end of the day. Emily came to school with a bruise on her arm where finger marks could visibly be seen. Emily's communication could not have been clearer, but I missed what she was trying to communicate. Now that the boyfriend is no longer in the picture, Emily is

happy, and the crying and screaming has ceased. I apologized
to Emily for not understanding what she was communicating to me. I have learned the valuable lesson not to dismiss
any "behavior" as anything less than a "communication"!

Please appreciate that it is incumbent upon every parent,
caregiver, and supporter to *exhaust* all possible avenues in offering those persons without a voice, like Emily, access to speech
alternatives. Curiously, Emily's teachers attempt to elicit her
speech by directing her to discern, and verbally identify, random objects placed before her, such as a book or a spoon.
She always indicates the wrong object, apparently deliberately; but, with Mollie's prompting, Emily cheerfully gets her
own spoon when it's time to eat!

Do not believe that your child is incapable of communicating, or even reading—despite what you may have been
told. Do start pursuing communication opportunities *now*. It
is urgent.

What follows are some areas to explore in partnership
with your child. Allow her to guide you to what makes
sense, what feels comfortable, and what works to her best
advantage. Remember, this is your child's decision to make;
and regardless of whether she can articulate some language
or not, you'll know soon enough which mode (or modes) of
speech alternatives will be of service to her.

A total communication approach offers myriad options,
depending upon the environment, the circumstances, and
the needs of the child. The options may be offered singularly or in tandem with one another. In this way, your
child will use what she likes because it gets her needs met.

Unused approaches may be faded out in favor of placing greater emphasis on what works. The goal is not necessarily to develop speech—if it's meant to come, rest assured, it'll come—the goal is to provide your child with an array of alternatives to speech to supplement any present vocalizations. Speech-language pathologists, occupational therapists, communication specialists, and other professionals accessed through your local school district, university, or special needs service providers may be able to provide insight, further information, or training relevant to any of the following aspects of communication.

Reading

Read everything and anything to your child, and do not stop until he starts reading to you instead (if your child isn't wired for speech, you've got a lifetime of reading enjoyment ahead of you both). And read material to your child at his chronological age level or beyond, *not* at the age level at which you've been told he "functions." *Challenge* his intellect. Do you know how many adults with autism I meet who are being offered age-inappropriate reading material such as children's storybooks? If we're presuming intellect, this makes no sense.

Read *with* your child, not *to* him; in other words, allow him to see the pictures, to turn the pages, and to follow the words. Ask him to point to objects or portions of the illustrations, or even to indicate a word or words by pointing (or allow your child to take your hand and use it to point as an extension of his own hand if manual dexterity is difficult for him).

If your child loves plants and flowers, get horticulture books out of the library to read together; if your child likes insects, look through *National Geographic* with her and read aloud the captions; and if your child seems drawn to outer space, look up astronomy Web sites with him, and read about his favorite planets. Also keep your child up to date on current events by reading from the newspaper with him every day (I prefer *USA Today* for its emphasis on colorful, eye-catching graphics). Infuse your child with reading material throughout each day.

Any number of my adult friends with autism who communicate by typing have shared that they *taught themselves* how to read at three and four years old when everyone around them thought it futile because they were deemed "retarded." They learned from *Sesame Street* or by surreptitiously studying stray newspapers and magazines left unattended. Do you think your child is absentmindedly engaging in *self-stimulatory behavior,* or *stimming,* by sitting with a book or magazine and swiftly leafing through each page, seemingly unaware?

One friend with autism, who does not speak, typed, "You read one sentence at a time. I read a *page* at a time." This revelation certainly puts ability and aptitude into perspective, doesn't it?

Pictures

Another option is to employ small, discreet photos of desired activities, people, animals, and places. The photos are the property of the individual and should be maintained by her in a portable booklet or binder. This communication option will have meaning only if you partner with your child to fill the binder with photos that stretch well beyond the basics, so start with her most passionate of interests to create an incentive to use it (learn more about passions in Chapter Seven).

Use real photographs wherever possible. Many official icon programs, available at a cost, have line drawings that are confusing or open to interpretation. For instance, an image for brushing one's teeth was of a face with no facial features except a huge gaping mouth with enormous horse teeth into which was inserted a toothbrush—it looked like the Alien! Instead, a clear photograph of your child brushing her teeth or an image of her toothbrush at your bathroom sink will work best.

Portable photos are a great start to provide one means of communication but they are also limited to what we *think* someone wants or even needs to tell us; photos can't possibly capture all that the highly intelligent, perfectly competent individual with autism is thinking or desires to express. Most often, people who are unpresuming of intellect construct picture communication systems to convey basic needs: choices of what to eat or drink, choices of activities (play a board game or bounce a ball?), or self-care skills like taking a bath and using the toilet—necessary, yes, but if you believe in a competence intact, this approach is severely limiting and potentially insulting. Think big, go with your child's passions, and challenge her intellect at her chronological age level or above! One young boy for whom I consulted had a huge binder of pictures that portrayed essential needs but he confided to me privately by typing, "My book does not help me to learn about life."

Technology

Assistive technology from desktop and laptop computers and computer programs to small, handheld communication devices should be explored in seeking the right match that suits each individual's needs, motor capacity, and comfort level. An Internet search using the words "assistive" or "augmentative communication" will yield any number of Web sites with a vast array of truly amazing technology, some of which qualifies as small, discreet, and portable.

Display screens, voice output devices, photo and video capacity, and computer capability are only some of the features. Voice activation or physical adaptations, like head-mounted laser pointers, are possibilities for personalizing equipment. Additionally, assistive technology expos may be held in your area or within driving distance. Your child's special education personnel should be knowledgeable resources about assistive technology: how to access it at low or no cost, how to use it on a trial basis, and where to go in order to have your child assessed for using such equipment (as well as test it out).

Oftentimes assistive technology is outrageously expensive (remember, we're talking about an industry), and you may have been challenged in engaging local resources, so consider beginning with your own ingenuity in the interim. Your child with autism may have already demonstrated a proclivity for using the computer—even without anyone showing him how. There are so many Internet sites filled with puzzles, games, and interactive activities, some associated with characters your child may recognize and enjoy. Also take advantage of using the computer with your child as a time when you and he can interact with one another.

Even if your child does not speak, he may be a fluent and articulate typist. If you really want a straight answer from your computer-literate child, send him an e-mail and request that he respond within twenty-four hours. You'll get a reply, and you might just be surprised at the depth of the insightful prose and the economy of the direct-and-to-the-point language you receive. Why would this method of communication be so effective? For the following reasons:

- Your child has been granted process time to thoughtfully compose a response.
- Your child is not pressured to interpret tough-to-discern nonverbal aspects of communication, such as facial expressions or body language.
- Your child isn't distracted by the color of your blouse, what's going on in the background behind you, or by an expectation to make direct eye contact.
- Your child can be more thorough and introspective in responding than he can if he feels compelled to say something in the moment just to give you an answer or to please you with what you want to hear (which may not be accurate).

Signing

Oftentimes verbalizations can come in conjunction with learning sign language, and if this is emphasized, signing is surely a valuable communication support. This will be most likely to occur if the signs being learned are motivating for your child because they are relevant, hold great importance, or are linked to his most passionate of interests. But please be very cautious about teaching sign language as the *sole mode* of communication. Sign language is not universally understood in our communities, so fluency outside a small circle of supporters is not possible. (In other words, your child would never be able to order a meal in a neighborhood restaurant using only sign language.) Additionally, professional providers of services that promote sign language as an exclusive mode of communication have an obligation, despite staff turnover, to ensure that all workers are as proficient in its use as the person being supported. However, this service often becomes a disservice because such continuity rarely occurs, and the person using sign language is left without a mode of communication during such downtimes. However, if the individual has a history *with family and friends* of using some select signs, please preserve this method of communication because it's familiar *and* it's working—even the made-up, homemade signs that are understood only by familiar folks can be useful this way.

When using appropriate sign language as a communication option, consider pairing or combining it with other modes of communication. For instance, you might point to the jar of peanut butter, saying the words "peanut butter" and using the sign for peanut butter simultaneously, while preparing a snack of peanut butter crackers with your child.

The Song's the Thing

If your child is working to produce some kind of vocalization that resembles speech, follow these three strategies: (1) praise her for her amazing efforts; (2) if you truly don't understand what she's saying, do not patronize her (don't say, for example: "Oh yeah? . . . Really? . . . That's nice!"), but do acknowledge the vocalization as communication ("I can't understand what you're saying but I love hearing the sound of your voice"); and (3) *go with it* by finding ways to draw out more of that good stuff! When in doubt, build upon your child's most passionate of interests.

I've known people who couldn't talk but could sing *beautifully*. Music is a very powerful and universal form of communication—there's magic in its purview to touch us all. Use it as another way in, another way to connect; just be certain that it's not your music played at your volume but your *child's* music played at a volume that is tolerable and pleasing for her.

I have yet to meet a person on the autism spectrum, particularly someone who lives in silence, for whom music is not lifeblood; it's that important! Whenever a person has suggested otherwise, it's been because someone else was playing music not enjoyed or appreciated by the individual with autism and playing it at an intolerable volume.

As you'll read later on, it is not uncommon for some individuals who do not speak to be drawn to certain genres of music, to particular musical artists with whom they can relate, or to certain songs or song lyrics. This is a form of symbolic communication, like the communication that transpired some years back when a young mother was being pressured to institutionalize her toddler son with autism. At the time, Madonna's song "Papa Don't Preach" was popular on the radio, and every time it played, this boy would pull himself up in his playpen and try in earnest to gain his mom's attention.

At first she thought he was just swaying and making noise to the music, but then it finally clicked—he was using the song lyrics as his own words when Madonna sang about making up her mind—she was *keeping her baby*! The mother correctly interpreted the communication, made the right decision, and kept her young son at home instead of sending him to live in an institution. The boy's intellect was not only evident in his clever, advanced use of the lyric but in the fact that he certainly overheard and understood a lot of the emotional turmoil about his future placement.

Similarly, I was once doing a consultation in a family's home for a seven-year-old boy with autism who was challenged by articulating speech. Looking at him, I asked him to tell me about his connection to music, something I sensed was true of him. He looked at me, smiled—then got up and left the room! But he came back shortly thereafter, having gone to his bedroom to retrieve a portable electronic keyboard that he proceeded to play for my entertainment.

I next asked him to *sing* for me—and he did, singing with great care and with measured enunciation that demonstrated his desire to communicate. And the song he chose was one he had learned in school about friendship! He selected a song about the importance of relationships in the context of having friends. It was a lovely moment for his family, and I further recommended that they draw out more of his speech by narrating everything they did—every interaction and household function—and singing these comments as often as they could. Before long, their son was articulating more verbalizations *and* his relationships with his parents and siblings were enriched more than ever.

Facilitated Communication

Facilitated communication (FC) is a communication technique that builds upon safe and trusting relationships. Through FC, an individual with autism, who does not speak or who has an inconsistent ability to articulate speech, pairs with a communication partner who has been properly trained in applying the FC technique.

The communication partner sits or stands next to the individual with autism and physically supports her by touching her hand, wrist, elbow, or shoulder to provide the confidence she requires to be calm, to focus, and to make the brain-body connections necessary to use her hand and arm. You will recall that one analogy for feeling autistic is those instances when your arm falls asleep during the night, precluding your ability to use it functionally because it is immobile and feels like lead; in the instance of FC, the communication partner is supporting the person to "awaken" the use of that arm.

If the person with autism is capable of isolating an index finger to point, she may be steadied by the communication partner and supported to touch in a downward motion to indicate a word or letters on a paper alphabet board, a picture, an object, or a key on a keyboard set before her. (Rather than pointing their own finger, some people may prefer to use the communication partner's hand to point, or perhaps to use an object, such as a pencil, instead.) The communication partner *does not* lead the person or make choices for her in this way and, actually, provides upward resistance, creating some physical tension as the person being supported to use FC pushes downward. This mild physical tension creates a measure of control for the person who is working to awaken the brain-body connection and ensures that she is moving to touch a communication of her choosing; if the tension were absent, the person with autism might run the risk of making unreliable communications, in the same way you likely would if someone intended for you to handwrite legibly while using your arm that was asleep. I can appreciate the skepticism of the casual observer, because, to the uninitiated, it *looks* like the facilitator is moving the individual's hand, but with proper training in the FC technique, this should not be occurring.

As the person with autism becomes more proficient and accustomed to the physical sensation, or rhythm, of the FC technique, the amount of physical support offered by the communication partner may fade to a lighter touch or eventually progress from the hand to the elbow to the shoulder. Independence free of physical support is the ultimate outcome of FC, but this can take years depending upon the person and her relationship with the communication partner(s). Still, aside from learning to speak or handwrite, or mastering two-handed typing, FC is a communication option that doesn't have the boundaries of pictures or of the preprogrammed devices that rely on content defined by what others believe the individual with autism wants to say. A good Internet resource for learning more about FC is the Web site of the Facilitated Communication Institute at Syracuse University: http://soeweb.syr.edu/thefci.

FC is not for everyone, but that decision should be one of informed choice on the part of each individual. I have certainly offered FC to individuals who seemed totally (and repeatedly) disinterested. Is it misused and misapplied? You bet. I have trained professionals to use FC since the 1990s, and for quality assurance, I ensure that they apply it to me (role-playing the person with autism) with the person being trained taking the part of the communication partner, and vice-versa. I have felt some of the people being trained, instead of supplying the previously referenced physical tension, actually move my hand instead. If this were not a simulation but an actual FC interaction with a person with autism, they would have—intentionally or unintentionally—risked improperly manipulating the person's communications. Mastering FC requires comprehension of the *technique*.

To further illustrate, I once observed a mother and daughter using FC. The daughter had significant physical limitations, could not ambulate independently (and used a stroller-type device), had limited use of her arms, and could not lift her head. The mother stood above her, with one hand supporting her daughter's hand, which was reaching up to a small, portable alphabet board that the mother held in her other hand. As I watched, this girl's finger pointed with lightening speed all over the board and, a few times, it appeared as though the mother shifted the board she was holding. Do I believe that the child, who could not lift her head to see what she was allegedly typing, was using FC? Absolutely not—and the mother was demonstrating bad FC form. That's not to say they didn't share a strong bond, and communicated in other ways; it's just that legitimate FC wasn't one of them in my opinion.

People may also be skeptical because an individual has reportedly lied, sworn, or communicated something with which these people disagreed while using FC. Guess what? People are people; and people lie, swear and may say things others don't like no matter who they are, even if it "seems" out of character.

Some of the most brilliant and wise individuals I know are folks with autism who use FC because they live in silence, carefully thinking, processing, and observing. For them, FC is a more eloquent, fluent alternative to speech, and they are best able to fully express themselves in writing, as may be true of some of us.

Remember that the ultimate outcome of FC is to achieve independence free from physical touch, as Sue Rubin showed us all in the Academy Award–nominated documentary *Autism Is a World*. And I do know others who are either *typing independently* or with very minimal physical support, such as a touch at the shoulder or elbow, among them are self-advocates like Amanda Baggs, Richard Attfield, and Jamie Burke. My friend Wally Wojtowicz used FC but, given an advanced stage of ALS (Lou Gehrig's disease), he has graduated to using a head-mounted laser pointer that tracks his eye gaze as he glances at a computer screen to communicate his thoughts about those who would disdain and disparage FC, indicating his own form of exacting retaliation.

> Reaching out to my very devoted family was easy because they saw the faint spark of intelligence that was masked from everyone else who believed that I was incapable of thought and incapable of learning anything more than one would try

to teach a dog. Time might heal in some cases, but, in others, time only perpetuates ideas, especially if they are without merit. . . . Yet, I will now tell you with a smile on my face that, at times, I would know which of a person's "buttons" to push to exasperate him or her and take advantage of autism's definition as a shield to hide behind, but only on rare occasions.

I have dear friends who are all too willing to introduce FC to disbelievers, and when I have availed this offer to my dissenters, they have all declined. They will also cite the studies that have disproven FC, while conveniently overlooking the studies in peer-reviewed journals that *have* proven FC's efficacy as a legitimate and viable communication technique. This leads me to suspect that there exists a fear of the unknown and an unwillingness by some professionals to relinquish control by adopting a presumption of intellect in persons believed to be mentally retarded. Does relinquishing control and trusting that FC may be authentic and of service to some mean we will finally be compelled to really listen to what people with autism are telling us? I certainly hope so.

Symbolic Communication

We know that it is imperative to determine alternatives to speech for each person without a voice, but what do we do in the interim? Part of supporting those without a viable means of communication means being good detectives, if not good archeologists, in deciphering *symbolic* communication.

Remember your little colony of nonspeaking coworkers? Think about how you'd react out of exasperation because no one was getting your pseudo-charades. Would you yell and scream in frustration, throw something, bang your head against the wall, or physically move against the folks who weren't understanding it?

If these things were done by someone with autism, we'd immediately label such outpourings as stereotypical behaviors when, in fact, we're not talking about behavior; we're talking about a function of *communication*—communication that cannot, in that moment, be expressed in ways that are effective, reliable, and universally understandable.

Which would you prefer: (1) that people ascribe your outburst to being unable to communicate any other way, or (2) that people ascribe your outburst to your presumed level of intellect (after all, isn't that how you're *supposed* to react when you have an intellectual impairment)?

For example, judged solely by their behavior, it's easy to conclude that a lot of people with some form of autism love and adore food. Friends and family may have had to consult with dieticians or nutritionists to better tailor (and taper) menus for these individuals, or people have had to monitor caloric intake because they know how much people with autism just love to eat! I and others have even had to caution some individuals to slow down at mealtimes because they can't seem to satiate themselves quickly enough.

On occasion, a child or teen may even have devoured an entire freshly baked confection (usually with chocolate) left unattended on a kitchen counter. Is this a *behavior*, or is it a symbolic *communication*? Well, if we consider it the former, think about the process of eating in the context of the lives people with autism may lead. Adults who have lived in congregate settings, such as institutions or group homes, may have learned to wolf down their meals so someone else doesn't raid their portion first. But food is also about the only *daily pleasure* many people have to look forward to. Many individuals with autism are without the social pressures neurologically conventional people suffer surrounding weight and appearance. So these individuals' drive to seek food is purely for pleasure, because it *feels good* (some people who are depressed often use food as an antidote).

Consuming food is a holistic process that involves *all* the senses. More than nourishment, it is a communal process that reminds us we are human. It is pleasurable and gratifying on many levels. In the context of decoding symbolic communication, we may wonder: does an individual with autism desire to eat because she's hungry, or because it fills a void in a sometimes colorless world?

Among other benign examples, I've deciphered that the toy tractors, trains and trucks that grown men with mental retardation supposedly "played with" (because, well, they were grown men with mental retardation) were actually symbolically linked to loved ones in their past who had direct affiliation with those vehicles. These men were using the toy vehicles as a way to call up memories of happy childhood times riding with people who loved them unconditionally and without judgment.

Behavior as Communication

As you may be, I am routinely appalled by the national and local news stories of children and adults with different ways of being who are abused. This abuse includes the overuse and misapplication of restraints. People with autism, of varying types and degrees, have been suffocated, locked in rooms, have had their arms and legs tied, and have been manipulated with the equivalent of electric cattle prods. School children have been strapped to chairs with mouths duct-taped shut, pinched, bitten (yes, by teachers), and locked in closets.

If you think such abuses are largely things of the past, go to neurodiversity.com (www.neurodiversity.com/abuse.html) or Children Injured by Restraint and Aversives (http://users .1st.net/cibra/index.htm) and review some of the recent headlines about abuse from around the country.

I was once asked to consult for a team that was challenged in supporting Jeffrey, an eighteen-year-old young man with autism. At home Jeffrey was strapped to a chair with a belt, but at school such control measures were limited because such a procedure could be interpreted as abusive in limiting his movement. The team had taken to videotaping his physical aggression during the day while he attended school in order to have some documentation for his out-of-control "behavior."

The team, which consisted of Jeffrey's parents, classroom teacher, various support staff, and school principal, sent me several such tapes prior to our first meeting to convince me of the seriousness of the situation. After viewing portions of these tapes, I chose to focus on a very few moments of one scene. In it, Jeffrey is seated with his teacher and they are quietly paging through a magazine together.

So far so good, until the teacher turns away from him to address a classroom aide and says to that aide, "Oh, by the way, I won't be here tomorrow morning and if Jeffrey isn't on his best behavior until I get back, deny him his library privileges."

Pow! Jeffrey suddenly clobbered the teacher with a punch to the jaw, seemingly out of the blue.

When I sat with the team, I began the meeting by playing that one brief portion of video and asking the team members to tell me what they saw. Initially they all responded by assuring me that what I saw was typical of Jeffrey's behaviors. I rewound the tape and played it again, requesting that they begin to deconstruct it in detail, which they did. Some team members thought that maybe Jeffrey was having a "bad morning." I again rewound the tape and continued rewinding it for the next half hour until finally—and fortunately—the understanding about exactly what happened came from the teacher herself, when she bravely confessed, "I shouldn't have talked about him that way in front of him. It was the first time he heard of my change of plans, and I presupposed that, in my absence, there would be trouble." Jeffrey was reacting in a clear, direct, and no-frills manner to communicate, "I'm angry at you for treating me so disrespectfully."

Jeffrey actually had many other moments of being quite sweet and gentle. But another "behavioral" issue the team wanted "fixed" was that Jeffrey was now customarily coming into school every morning, climbing up on a desktop, getting on all fours, beating his stomach, and screaming and moaning. I knew this wasn't a behavior, it was a symbolic communication—something that in the moment couldn't be expressed in any other way. Knowing that many people with autism have very delicate digestive systems, I advised the team to rule out any gastrointestinal issues. After a thorough examination at the hospital, it was discovered that Jeffrey had a lower gastrointestinal tract bacterium that was eating him alive from the inside out—he had been in *pain*. Once treated with antibiotics, his "behavior" of climbing onto the desktop and screaming was cast off and did not return. For further measure, I advocated that a milk substitute be used on his morning cereal as it seemed that an apparent lactose intolerance had exacerbated his gastrointestinal issues.

In another instance, Brad, who had once been both restrained and locked in a closet due to his behaviors, became ballistic over cracks in floors, walls, and ceilings. To most caregivers, this would seem irrational and typical of behavior attributed to someone who is autistic and mentally retarded. It was deeper than that; in collaboration with Brad's team members, we deduced that Brad's aversion to cracks was symbolic, linked to the one impression burned into his memory during all the hours he had, years prior, spent terrified and alone, locked in a pitch-black closet: the thin, white crack of light that shone through just under the door.

Oftentimes interpreting symbolic communication is like fitting together puzzle pieces: cracks in floors, walls, and ceilings + unresolved trauma + feelings of worthlessness and inadequacy + no trust in the limits of caregivers = triggers of reactive communication.

In Brad's case, decoding symbolic communication didn't solve everything, and that outcome is typical. Many folks have outstanding, long-term mental health issues that have gone undiagnosed, misdiagnosed, or mistreated for years. We also need to support each individual in a holistic approach that takes into account all facets of her life. However, understanding silent communications can be a powerful preventive diffuser.

I also consulted for David, a young man who was routinely restrained in his community home because of his acts of physical aggression. David's situation was a classic instance of the *high-maintenance person*. He had broken the noses, arms, and car windows of his staff, and he was kicked out of his day program. David's quality of life had deteriorated to the bare essentials, and his home was Spartan at best: a mattress on the floor, a television bolted to the floor, and nothing on the walls. He indicated that he wanted to eat alone as much as possible, and then only using paper and plastic plates and utensils. He also had the habit of becoming enraged if there were no apples in the house. Much to the chagrin of his caregivers, he insisted upon holding an apple in each hand and would sniff and lick them excessively before consuming them. He would react violently if anyone tried to remove them or offer a substitute.

Perhaps you've already correctly guessed that David wanted paper plates and cups when taking his solitary meals as a preventive measure to ensure the safety of all—a brilliant but unrecognized bit of self-advocacy. Like the toy trucks played with by grown men, the apples also held a connection to David's past. He was estranged from his mother but during the time he had lived with her, he had subsisted on a diet full of raw, fresh vegetables and fruit, including lots of . . . apples! His team acknowledged that his mother was the one person in life he truly loved. Being without a photo album, home movies, or any other personal item linked to mother, David used the scent and taste of apples to switch his mind-movies into operation; movies that replayed happy, loving memories. The apples were a tangible means through which to communicate symbolically his desire to reunite with mother. She was all David had, he believed.

Finally, Meg, a middle-aged woman, had the unenviable habit of constantly pressing on her bladder and making herself urinate—something she did not do prior to relocating from the state center (in which she had resided for most of her life) to her community residence. Everyone assumed this was an "attention-seeking behavior," and one person rightly speculated that it might be sexually related in that Meg might've been intentionally manipulating her body to achieve a needed physical release. After ensuring that Meg was clear of any urinary tract infection, I supported her team in deconstructing the process of Meg's bladder pressing in a symbolic way.

We discussed it step by step: what happens (you wet yourself); what do you get (release, warmth, scent); and what might it symbolize? We realized that everything that had enabled Meg to feel safe and comfortable and at home had been uprooted. *But,* she had never been without urine, and the warmth and scent it brought was a constant, symbolic way of staying grounded in an unfamiliar and strange environment. *She was homesick for the state center!*

Tactics for Communication

What can we do to better enhance our understanding of the ways in which people who don't speak might communicate? Here are a few suggestions; perhaps you and your child's support team can brainstorm others.

- Presume intellect, and interact with a belief in competence regardless of your child's supposed intellectual differences. Strategize *discreet* ways of communicating very sensitive or potentially humiliating information about your child without doing it in front of him (this includes communicating with physicians and other community professionals) by phoning, faxing, or e-mailing sensitive information in advance.

- Don't jump to conclusions and don't accept what you see at face value; often there's something deeper lying just below the surface. Do your homework by exploring the symbolic content of silent communication both on your own and by consulting with other family members or people who know and work with your child.

- Provide your child with kind and gentle assurances that you will attempt to respectfully understand her "language."

Regularly brainstorm the most challenging of silent communications with your child, your spouse, and whenever possible, your child's educators or other professionals *as a team*. Deciphering symbolic communication does not have to fall to any one person; the input of all should be welcomed and valued. Pursuing viable means of establishing independence in your child's ability to communicate is the single most important thing you can endeavor, even if it's as simple as pointing to index cards marked "yes" and "no." Through communicating independently, she will demonstrate her intellect, be better able to convey her wants and needs, and be poised to advocate for herself without dependency on others.

CHAPTER FIVE

Your Child's Acute Sensitivities

As an autism consultant, I am often asked if I believe in behavior management; that is, a rigid program that drills children into compliance for hours on end. My response is yes, I believe in behavior management, *but* I believe in managing the behavior of *everyone around* the individual with autism so that they come to understand the autistic experience in all its mystery, simplicity, and great beauty, because I teach from an *inside-out perspective*, meaning from the perspective of understanding the individual through his or her eyes. It is a form of intercession, or go-between, to act as an interpreter for those who have made assumptions or bought into stereotypes about autism. My role, like that of yours as a parent, is to create an awareness, appreciation, and understanding that cultivates a transformation for those who do not see the individual with autism in a humanistic light.

In so doing, and as you've read, I don't talk about "behavior," I talk about "communication," specifically, discerning and decoding the function of that communication. This is particularly important when considering the sensory sensitivities of young people with autism, attention deficit disorder (ADD), attention deficit/hyperactivity disorder

(ADHD), obsessive-compulsive disorder (OCD), and other experiences. Let's remember, too, that many exquisitely sensitive children may not realize they're enduring anything any different from anyone else; and some may not have the language or verbal skills to fully express what's going on. Instead it may come out—and it's got to come out—through communication that gets mislabeled as noncompliant, aggressive tantrums, or "meltdowns." In my opinion, and in my experience, this can be traced to one or a combination of communication challenges that get mistaken for "autistic behaviors." Let's now revisit these challenges, which you first read about in Chapter Three, in greater depth:

- The inability to communicate in ways that are effective, reliable, and universally understandable. (Think about how it felt if you've ever had laryngitis, couldn't speak, and relied upon others to second-guess you.)
- The inability to communicate physical pain and discomfort in ways that are effective, reliable, and universally understandable. (Think about the last time you endured significant or chronic pain, and consider what it would be like if you couldn't tell someone.)
- The inability to communicate issues of mental wellness in ways that are effective, reliable, and universally understandable. (What if you had no voice to express the last time you felt depressed, irritable, and disinterested in being with others?)

The phrase "inherently gentle and exquisitely sensitive" may best describe the autistic experience. The acute sensitivity that correlates to all five senses, in various combinations depending on the given individual, can cause a person's nervous system to vibrate at a different frequency from what is considered typical. The communication impediments in the foregoing list may be linked to feeling overwhelmed, frustrated, or painful in response to sensory irritants in one's environment from which there is no relief. We have already explored communication in depth and in the forthcoming sections, we will also acknowledge issues of pain (including sensory sensitivities) and mental wellness as they relate to communication needs and expressions.

Take what you know to be true of your own sensory experiences—the tactile sensation and goose-pimple feeling when you've pulled apart cotton balls, for example—and bump it up a dozen notches (at least), and you may be vibrating up in the stratosphere with the intensity of many people with autism. This may predispose such individuals to perceive all things seen and unseen, and to filter out few of the environmental stimuli that the average person screens out naturally.

When someone autistic is exposed to overwhelming stimuli in his home, educational, vocational, and community environments—stimuli that *assault* his sensory sensitivities—this exposure generates severe pain, which may or may not be expressed. As I'm suggesting, how it is expressed outwardly may be misinterpreted as blowouts, tantrums, or meltdowns. It cannot help but cause physical impairment, even literally impeding a person's ability to move forward. Over time, this can also contribute to the erosion one's mental health if relief and compassionate understanding are not availed.

We must be thoughtful, gentle, and sensitive in how we help people with autism to be as successful as they can be in the home, school, workplace, and community. We must ensure that they have respite at intervals throughout the day. We must be in tune to the sensory sensitivities of individuals in the ways they are supported. What follows is further explanation, delineated by each of the senses.

Sight

Visual Thinkers and Learners

Many people on the autism spectrum (but not all) take in everything they see and filter out nothing. They tend to be detail people, such as spotting a small foreign object on the floor from across the room, or noticing some overlooked nuance in the background. Many think in visual streams of pictures and movies, and can recall and replay these images in their minutiae—these images include positive, loving experiences as well as traumatic ones.

Eye Contact or Not

Lack of eye contact does not mean the child with autism is not listening; absorbing a vast amount of detail increases the potential for distraction. Demanding direct eye contact may cause the child to be *less* attentive, because of the visual confusion of the human face in constant, abstract motion.

Specific Visual Stressors

Many people with autism "record" strong associative elements that are called up with visuals. Certain colors, for example, may cause distress that may be linked to disturbing experiences in the past.

Many children with autism have an extreme sensitivity to lighting, particularly artificial lighting (especially fluorescent or halogen lighting) but even intense sunlight can be a problem. Exposure to such lighting can be physically exhausting and draining. It can affect vision, causing it to be blurred; it can distort depth perception and a person's ability to move and ambulate.

Accommodations

Use natural lighting, less lighting, table or floor lamps, and filtering screens or offer visors or sunglasses or tinted (Irlen) lenses—although for some people the discomfort of the lighting may be preferable to that of the touch of something new against the skin.

Visual blocks, such as partitions or carrels in the classroom or workplace, can cut down on upsetting distractions. Minimizing classroom decor may decrease a student's anxiety, distractibility, and overstimulation.

Hearing

Unpredictable Noises

People's voices, coughing, laughing, and sneezing; dogs barking; sirens and fire alarms going off; babies or other children screaming or crying; vacuum cleaners roaring; lights and fans humming—these sounds may be startling and assaultive. They cannot always be *predicted*. But in the home, educational, or vocational environment there can be greater control.

Children who are bothered by sound sometimes turn up the volume of their music or television. There's a difference between loud sounds made by others and loud music or noise that the child perpetuates, chooses, and controls. *It's her music*, not someone else's. This should not be misinterpreted as willful misconduct or inconsistency of behavior.

Accommodations

Something inserted in the ear canal, like earplugs, is usually not well tolerated. We can instead offer headphones or a Walkman or iPod that plays soothing music selected by the individual. In school and workspace environments, classical music played softly in the background can help people with autism to focus and concentrate.

Smell and Taste

Gag or Vomit Reactions

Some kids react with gagging or vomiting at the sight or smell of certain foods. Some children's palates are so sensitive that certain foods and food textures are intolerable; these range from soft or slimy foods (such as Jell-O and pudding) to crunchy textures (such as celery and carrots or crunchy-style peanut butter). Resistance to foods may also be associated with memories (such as forced feeding of food) or with painfulness in the mouth and throat.

Food Allergies

Allergies can be culprits that induce pain and discomfort; typical allergens in foods are dyes, preservatives, casein (dairy), and gluten (wheat and other grains). Gastrointestinal pain can manifest itself in behavior that may not appear to be linked to digestive problems. In discerning what is being communicated, it is crucial to first rule in or rule out physical pain or discomfort.

Accommodations

Consult with a dietician and nutritionist to assess the diet of your child and partner with that person to factor in or out substitutes for the foods that cause distress. Don't get caught up in power struggles around food in the name of normalization. Children will sample other foods if and when they choose, though you should continue to make a range of choices available.

Touch

Clothing Textures

Skin can be exquisitely sensitive. Children might be limited in the types of fabric that their skin can tolerate, such as cotton. Clothes that feel fine to the average person might need to be washed repeatedly to soften them; tags might need to be cut out. Sometimes used clothing is preferable, because it has a long history of being worn.

Don't get caught up in power struggles around clothing, compelling kids to wear clothes they reject and interpreting their communication through rejection as "noncompliance."

Listen to words and conduct that communicate things like "these clothes scratch." People with autism are often inherently blatant and direct. If someone says clothes scratch, it is because they do; figure out where and why and take measures to make them right.

Unwelcome Touch

Be respectful of people's personal space; we so often trespass a child's personal space because, well, she's a child. In supporting a kid with differences, we want to feel reciprocation of the love and care we are demonstrating. It is there, but the child with autism may not rush to greet you or embrace you. The child may turn or go rigid or push you away, because your touch may cause shock waves of an oversensitizing or desensitizing stimulus. Do not touch someone suddenly or from behind or without permission.

Await the *invitation in:* a subtle communication that it is acceptable to get closer. This may look like your child inching closer to the place where you are sitting or slowly extending a pinky in your direction or allowing you to touch a treasured object of his.

Deep-Pressure Touch

The same kids who do not welcome abrasive, unexpected touch may seek the weight of extra layers of clothing or may self-swaddle in comforters or burrow under cushions and mattresses. Some children even ask family members to sit on them! (Such individuals may have some hyposensitivities—be undersensitive in some ways—*and* still have acute hypersensitivities.) Deep-pressure sensation is a way to maintain focus, to decompress, to reorganize before reentering the sensory-insensitive world.

Extra layers of clothing or individually styled weighted vests (perhaps a hunting vest, instead of the stigmatizing vest sold specially for the disability market) can fill *temporary* deep-pressure needs in public.

Self-Regulating Activities

A repetitive action or activity, such as twirling a string, can be soothing in its tactile or visual self-controlled *sameness*. (In other words, the repetition is the same every time.) Often this calming coping strategy is mistakenly called self-stimulation, or *stimming*. Try using new language to describe self-*soothing* techniques. This is the proper response to such so-called behaviors.

Recommendations for Educators

Educators and support staff will wish to be just as understanding as parents are of the hypersensitivity of children with autism. If not, the child's daily focus becomes a matter of *survival* and not education.

- Staff must be aware of the sensory sensitivities of each child with autism.

     A lack of awareness means we are setting people up for failure. A checklist of sensory sensitivities needs to

be developed for kids with autism, and reviewed regularly (see the Appendix for one such form).

- Staff must develop courtesy and respect by removing or
diminishing sensory factors they contribute.

  They must assess themselves: hygiene (no odors on
  their breath from coffee or cigarettes, for instance), no
  distracting jewelry, no loose long hair (pull it back),
  no perfumes or colognes, no scented detergents.

  They must be sure to shop for foods that the child
  can tolerate, both to eat and to watch staff eat.

  They must pay attention to the volume and frequency of phones ringing, the public address system, and
  the volume and duration of television and radio sound.

Home, School, and Community Environments

In addition to understanding how the five senses can be
overstimulated, it is helpful to become aware of the sources
of stimulation in various environments in the spirit of *prevention* instead of *intervention*.

- Notice floor textures in living environments and the differences in light and reflections over time (how a room
appears at different times of day and night).
- Rethink community outings. Do not set children with
autism up for sensory overload: many cannot tolerate
fireworks, race cars, malls, or amusement parks and
would prefer a picnic, walk in the woods, sitting by
a pond, or visiting a farm or zoo.

- Scout environments *in advance* of going, especially doctors' offices. Gather information (especially visual information such as photos or videos) so the elements of a new environment can be anticipated. Practice *prevention* in the future, not intervention in the moment.

- Rethink traditional education environments in favor of creating separate spaces tailored to individual needs.

- Strategize low-cost solutions to observed issues. For example, where possible, do away with break buzzers and instead assign the child to walk around and tell people it's break time. Look at lighting adjustments such as using lamps or natural light; listen for noise of equipment, slamming doors, and blaring radios; put felt pads on the bottoms of chair legs to avert scraping noises; be mindful of allowing too many conversations. Sensitive children taking in these sensory details cannot work productively because they're concentrating on blocking out stimuli.

- Provide lots of opportunities to convey the educational curriculum visually and through computer technology.

Prevention Instead of Intervention

The ideas and techniques just summarized will be further explored in greater detail. Here's one real-life instance of putting into practice the previously recommended philosophy of *prevention instead of intervention*.

I once heard from a concerned grandmother who told me, "I love my grandson Andrew dearly, but when he comes to my house for holidays or family get-togethers, he only lasts about twenty minutes before he has a tantrum. How do I make him behave and still include him?"

I responded by thanking her for being such a caring and concerned grandmother as to want to include Andrew in family gatherings in her home. I went on to speculate that she'd been trying to learn about autism and, if so, she understood that most people with autism possess acute sensory sensitivities—specifically, a strong aversion to loud and unpredictable noise or bright lighting or food tastes and aromas that can be overwhelming.

Perhaps the most respectful way to reenvision this grandmother's inquiry is to reflect upon Andrew's sensory sensitivities using *our own* sensory sensitivities as a way of measurement. For instance, are there some kinds of music you simply don't appreciate? How would you feel if you were confined to an area and compelled to listen to heavy metal rock played at full volume? I bet you'd be "tantruming" in no time too!

Family gatherings are often loud, crowded, and unpredictable, with lots of overstimulating, overwhelming sensory sensations like simultaneous laughing, music, TV sound, and video games blaring, or foods that may make one so sensitive feel nauseated. After such occasions, don't you feel exhausted when everyone leaves too?

Instead of perceiving Andrew's "tantrums" as "autistic behaviors," his grandmother (and others around him) should try thinking of his reaction in terms of *communication*. It's not that he doesn't love his grandmother or that he's deliberately being bratty. He probably *wants to* comply and please everyone, but it's *too, too much!* Even though he speaks, it doesn't mean he recognizes his own sensory triggers or has a way to put language to them. All he knows is that he's feeling increasingly agitated and irritated and that making a scene works in that he gains relief and can leave the hurtful environment.

I told grandma that well before the next time Andrew's scheduled to visit, the two of them should make an agreement about family gatherings. To begin, she should tell him she understands and wants to help find a compromise. She could show him a safe, quiet space in her home that will be his alone when he visits. He can go there whenever he needs to. She might make available books, drawing materials, computer access, or whatever helps him to become absorbed in something to block out (temporarily) the hubbub of family.

Reunions and holidays can be stressful for all of us. Remembering to be especially sensitive to the needs of Andrew, and others like him, will aid us in making compassionate accommodations that will poise us all for successful and pleasant visits. This kind of strategy puts the focus on preventive measures to ensure success.

A Case of Tiptoeing

In another instance, a mom raised a question with me relating to the concept I mentioned earlier of hyposensitivity. Her question—one that's actually common among parents of children on the autism spectrum—concerned her daughter, who consistently walked on her toes. I'm glad to have the opportunity to address it here as I know it will hold relevance for this mother's daughter, Summer, as well as many other children with autism.

In my experience and in my opinion, there are two possibilities for Summer's toe walking. First, I asked her mom if she'd noticed that Summer had any acute sensory sensitivity to tactile sensations. For example, did she seem irritable wearing certain articles of clothing or particular fabrics against her skin? Did she tear tags out of her clothes, or prefer to go barefoot instead of wear socks? If so, her toe walking might have something to do with the delicate undersides of her feet and an uncomfortable sensitivity to making contact with the floor.

If that could be what's happening with Summer, her mother needs to consider the texture of the surfaces on which Summer is most likely to tiptoe. In thinking about other sensory sensitivities she might experience, does it make sense that certain floor surfaces might provoke a strong reaction in her? If so, what are the compassionate accommodations this mother might be able to make in adjusting and adapting the environment (such as putting natural-fiber throw rugs down over carpets or flooring with certain textures)? In some instances, children have actually had allergic reactions to synthetic fibers and chemicals in carpeting. Also, how might Summer gain some measure of control over her sensitivity in ways that flow naturally within typical daily routines? Would she enjoy playing with other children barefoot in a sandbox, or using differently textured sponges on the soles of her feet at bath time?

If this scenario sounds similar to what your own child is experiencing, you may wish to consult with both an occupational therapist and a physical therapist for ideas about adapting family routines to aid your child in having fun with family and friends while reducing his tactile sensitivity.

A second thought has to do with the autistic propensity for feeling disconnected from one's own limbs (arms, legs, trunk), and how they move in space, formally called *proprioception*. This sensation of uncertainty about one's body parts is frightening (remember the arm that fell asleep), and can also be related to delays in learning to use the toilet.

When you stand on tiptoe, you are *really* feeling your legs especially your calves—there's no disputing where they are, and that clear-cut sensation may actually be what gives Summer the confidence to propel forward and ambulate independently. For children like Summer who walk on tiptoe often, I always recommend a happy and fun exercise routine on a daily basis; not only are the health benefits evident, but stretching, squatting, and jumping (especially to favorite music) will open or establish neural pathways (brain-body connections) to help foster a working relationship with one's limbs and how they function properly. Better yet, get children like Summer moving *in water* (in a pool or even the bathtub), which will provide them with an overall pressure while giving natural resistance.

Without respectful, compassionate understanding of the acute sensory sensitivity needs of our children with autism, we may make the mistake of labeling outward expressions of pain and overload as severe behaviors. Please use the ideas communicated here as a starting point in your continued dialogue about best supporting the very sensitive child with autism.

Pain

The issue of pain, and pain that goes undetected, undiagnosed, and untreated or not properly treated, is an important one for us all; but perhaps it becomes even more complicated when discussing autism because of all the variables that may come to bear upon any single child's pain experience.

"Recovering" children from autism by alleviating their acute pain in the form of seizures, gastrointestinal issues, skin conditions, projectile vomiting, and other extreme and urgent health issues (attributed by some to toxins in vaccinations) has received a great deal of media attention lately, with headlines such as "Government Concedes Vaccine Injury Case," "Vaccines' Link to Autism Unclear," and "No Link Between Childhood Vaccine, Autism." I am uncertain whether those children whose development was arrested or regressed (and later recovered) due to such reactions experienced true autism, or if they presented outwardly with *autistic-like symptoms* due to the loss of speech, fine and gross motor skills, and self-care skills. Nonetheless, the devastating and impairing impact of pain on the nervous system of your exquisitely sensitive child should not go underestimated.

Think on the last time you were in significant pain. It affected your mood, your conduct, and your interactions with others. But where the person with autism is concerned, we tend to jump to conclusions about behaviors because of the autism label. Instead of perceiving someone's extreme conduct as "attention-seeking behavior," the responsible measure to take would be to rule out (or in) real pain and discomfort.

If pain is eventually discovered or identified, your first thought might be to ask why you didn't notice it, or why your child didn't simply convey it in an understandable manner. I have some thoughts for your consideration on why your child's pain may go unreported, and I'd like to share them with you here. I hope these autistic rationales will resonate for you as well as many other parents who are reading and wondering similarly.

Your child may not have reported his pain because

- He may not be neurologically wired for speech, or—even if he does speak—he may not have a way to describe or put language to what he's experiencing in the moment.

- He may have a flat affect—that is, an expressionless facial appearance that doesn't seem to register much of any emotion, making him tough to "read."

- His brain may not be properly registering the pain signals his body is sending it because of neurological crossed wires, so to speak; or he may have a high pain threshold or a delay in processing pain.

- He may not know there's a parental expectation that he will tell someone if he's in pain (you may have to teach this concept to him). Or he may not know how much pain he should feel before telling someone.

- He may have an extreme fear of doctors, especially if he's been treated roughly or insensitively in ways that were not respecting of his personhood. This makes allowing the pain to go unreported the lesser of two evils.

- Similarly, he may have had an adverse reaction when previously given pain medication, so he now chooses to say nothing to avoid repeat circumstances.

- He may not realize that what he's experiencing is anything *different* from what anyone else feels (like the boy with autism who got relief from mild asthma only at age eight and then exclaimed, "I didn't know it wasn't supposed to hurt when I breathe!").

- He may be trying to manage the pain independently but his effort looks like self-injurious activity (such as head banging)—that is, he's creating *another* pain as a diversion from the initial pain felt.

In a number of instances the pain experienced by people with autism is linked directly to gastrointestinal issues that are untreated or unresolved. In particular, as previously noted, an acute sensitivity to dairy- and wheat-based food products, the proteins and enzymes of which do not digest properly and, instead, leak through the stomach lining into the bloodstream and affect how the brain regulates the body.

It is a myth and stereotype that "people with autism don't feel pain." That view almost supposes we're talking about individuals who are nonhuman, doesn't it! As you've just read, a variety of factors pertaining to pain may make sense when you reflect upon your child's experience. Above all else, please remember that we are all truly brothers and sisters of one another, and we are *all* more alike than we are different—whether we're in pain or feeling joyful elation.

Dealing with Related Psychological Concerns

When we think about actions that get labeled as "extreme autistic behaviors," we tend to think about one or any combination of the following:

- Hitting
- Kicking
- Biting
- Spitting
- Cursing
- Pulling hair
- Scratching
- Destroying property
- Urinating somewhere other than a toilet
- Throwing or smearing feces
- Doing harm to oneself (including head banging)
- Doing harm to others (physical aggression)

Let's be clear: regardless of what you've been led to believe, none of the preceding "behaviors" are clinical features of autism. In other words, these modes of conduct are rightfully interpreted not as behaviors but as *communications* separate from autism—a by-product of being inherently gentle and exquisitely sensitive and being unable to communicate or tell about physical pain or put language to mental health symptoms.

As I've suggested, a large percentage of the mothers of children with autism whom I meet are depressed. If you are depressed or anxious; abusive; or addicted to shopping, nicotine, sex, food, or illegal or prescription drugs, chances are your child is genetically vulnerable to being predisposed to mental health issues as well. Couple this with a family history of such experiences (on either side of the family) as well as your child's very sensitive physiology, and you might appreciate how common issues of psychological, emotional, and mental wellness may be in persons with autism, issues that are *separate* from being autistic.

Here's a good example. When I conduct private consultations for persons on the autism spectrum, I purposefully go in "cold." That is, I absolutely want to know *nothing* about the individual in advance save for his or her first name and age; the rest is superfluous for my purposes. After flying across the state where I live early one morning, I found that it was arranged for me to consult with the team (a parent, a teacher, a psychologist, and staff caregivers) for a seventeen-year-old young man named Chad. It was not until I was picked up at the airport, en route to the meeting, that I even understood we were headed to a psychiatric facility for juveniles. *Ninety percent* of my work has nothing to do with the individual; rather it has to do with transforming the support team's perceptions about him or her. But on this particular morning, wires got crossed, and it was believed I was there to observe Chad one on one exclusively.

I was seated in a waiting room area when they brought him to meet me: over six feet tall, well over 200 pounds, and nonverbal. Yet I presumed his intellect and spoke to him as my peer. I gently introduced myself and, given the early hour, I asked him if he'd had his breakfast. The staff person accompanying Chad said he had not, to which I replied with great sympathy, "Oh you poor thing, you must be so hungry. Can we please bring his breakfast here to him?"

Soon Chad's breakfast was brought in, and he sat across from me quickly consuming his orange juice, buttered toast, and Cheerios. Not once did he make direct eye contact with me, but nonetheless I continued communicating to him with loving compassion.

"Thank you so much for adjusting your schedule to meet with me. You know, I can tell just by looking at you that you're very smart inside," I said. "When you're finished eating, I'd like it very much if you'd come join me on the sofa here."

I didn't have to ask twice, and when Chad finished his meal, he wiped his mouth and sat next to me on the small, upholstered loveseat. I continued as I leaned closer, "Chad, I don't know what you were told about me, but I want to let you in on a secret. I'm not here for you. . . . I'm here for *them*. I'm here to teach them to see how very smart you are inside in the way that I see you."

Just then a curious thing happened. Chad grimaced and rubbed his eyes and wiped his cheeks: he was weeping. I put my arm around him and rubbed his back, and he rested his head on my shoulder. "I know, sweetheart, I know." I softly said. "Try to be strong and patient a little longer. I pledge to do my very best by you. I will not forget you, and I hope we will meet again one day soon."

As we got up, we hugged good-bye. Chad went back to his classroom and I went into the team meeting. What I later learned was that for the remainder of that day, Chad was happy and smiling. I also learned that he was the one kid in that facility no one wanted to get near because he had a reputation for being so violent and out of control.

What the Chads of the world need to know is

- You're not a bad boy (or girl or person);
- Yes, you have autism but that's not the issue—autism we can do;
- What you experience has a name; and
- It's not your fault.

My experience with Chad was confirmation of the three previously defined tenets that drive what gets mislabeled as "behaviors": being unable to communicate, being unable to communicate pain and discomfort, and being unable to communicate issues of mental wellness. As a result of the consultation, it was revealed that Chad had limited means with which to communicate, and such means were implemented inconsistently; his sensory sensitivities hadn't been considered; he had rampant diarrhea (likely diet related) and severe varicose veins on one of his testicles, which was also enlarged; he had significant allergies; and he had a Russian-roulette set of mental health diagnoses, none of which seemed like a good match (and which had been unsuccessfully treated, hence his out-of-home placement in the psychiatric facility). All of this led to what is probably a legitimate diagnosis of a mental health mood disorder, a disorder that is *separate from*, not a function of, Chad's autism.

It is imperative to correctly recognize all the different components of the experience of persons like Chad, otherwise these individuals risk a lifetime carousel of treatments, hospitalizations, and alternative living arrangements.

If your child routinely experiences extreme mood swings that include some (or all) of the preceding list of behaviors, especially self-injury, property destruction, or physical aggression against others, he may be considered at risk for the same kinds of treatment options as Chad experienced. But here is what *you* can do as your child's advocate to refrain from making a challenging situation worse. Apply these tenets until your child's mental health is clinically stable.

- *Create a predictable environment.* Reliable structure and dependable routines are a must in order for everyone to feel comfortable and grounded. Create a visual, mutually agreed upon schedule of activities each day, with as few surprises (last-minute changes) as possible.
- *Start low and go slow.* This means having, within the reliable structure, low pressure and low demands, for the time being.
- *No means NO.* Your child's communications of his mental stress *will* escalate the more you press and push your child to change his mind after he has made a choice or a decision and for as long as you won't take his no for an answer.
- *Business is NOT as usual.* Your child's mental state is extremely fragile, though it may not show outwardly in any given moment, and this knowledge should guide

expectations. Issues of mental health are intangible, so if it helps you, consider adopting the compassionate approach you'd take if your child were recovering from a *physical* illness, disease, or accident.

- *Keep it simple, subtle, interest-based.* Activities, choices, and community outings should reflect these three principles.

- *Use fewer words.* Be concise and direct in your verbal communications.

- *Use a calm, even tone of voice.* There is nothing to be gained by escalating in accordance with your child's meltdown.

- *Make the environment safe.* Safety-proof your home, and remove or lock up all firearms, sharp or pointed objects or anything glass, and ensure that cushions and pillows are always handy for use as buffers or shields.

- *Keep the environment calm.* No loud, simultaneous voices, radios, music, or TVs.

- *Minimize external environmental stimuli.* This means *no* outings to the mall, crowded restaurants, sports events, or family gatherings, for now.

- *Focus on the big picture.* Instead of rehashing specific incidents, think in terms of *symptoms,* not behaviors.

- *Offer affirmation of unconditional love.* Validate the inextinguishable love within a family united.

Many people with autism also grapple with acute anxiety. Often this can be traced to their having little or no control in self-determining activities or making even simple choices in their lives, and experiencing overwhelming anxiety due to the unpredictability of daily routines. This may result in waking up during the night and other sleep disturbances. These also tend to be the individuals who are constantly asking the same question over and over again in order to receive a consistent assurance that nothing's changed or been disrupted.

Suffice it to say, if your home is chaotic, disorganized, and absent any semblance of predictable structure, your child will be a product of his environment, and it will reflect outwardly in his conduct (I bear witness to this often). This is not something to then expect a professional to make better; creating proactive change starts with *you*.

Take Austin, for instance, who experienced anxiety reflective of a vastly disorganized home environment. The commonplace reaction would be to believe that his anxiety was a by-product of his autism and that it should be treated with medication (which may ultimately have long-term side effects). But the best way to quell, soothe, calm, and contain his anxiety and to benefit both him and his family turned out to be a picture schedule created and implemented in partnership with him in order to create a point of reference that could be used to orient him to the time and sequence of activities. When this schedule was arranged with Austin the night before (prior to bedtime) for the next day, his anxiety virtually dissipated.

Also included in such a schedule should be community choices that are sensory-friendly and without crowds (not the mall or the movies). Preferred activities, such as time on the computer or playing video games, may be regulated by having the child use a timer set to an agreed-upon and reasonable time frame. If you've ever misplaced or lost your PDA, daily planner, or appointment book, you may well appreciate the panic of uncertainty felt when one doesn't know what's coming next.

For similar reasons, Austin was paralyzed by severe storms. Acknowledging the unpredictability of weather and storm systems should also include some role or responsibility for Austin so that he can take charge and exert some measure of control. Even though weather is unpredictable, there is such a thing as *forecasting*, and perhaps by reading the paper, watching the news, or looking it up on the Internet, Austin could become his family's weatherman or report the weather each morning at school. This concept of instilling control in order to aid someone to feel safe and comfortable may be applied to many similar circumstances of anxiety, and it is a healthy and common-sense alternative to "Band-Aiding" the issue with medication or behavioral therapy, which doesn't address the true issue.

Fostering Autism Cultural Competency

You are perhaps aware of national news stories about children with autism being excluded from church, removed from airplanes, and kicked out of restaurants for "autistic behavior." From my perception, I presume—not the worst—but a conflict over neurodiversity, a lack of autism cultural competency, at the root of such incidents. These stories culminated perhaps most succinctly in a report brought to my attention about a radio talk-show host who referred to autism as a hoax, a fraudulent excuse for bad parenting, and who, not unlike any number of unenlightened laypersons, concluded that children with autism are "brats" and "idiots."

You can only know what you know—until you know better or at least differently. And remember, ignorance need not hold negative connotations if one endeavors a greater appreciation and respect. Autism is oftentimes an invisible disability, meaning, many of us with the more subtle autistic experiences get by, blend, and "pass" for normal because there's nothing particularly telling about our outward appearance at first glance. It is obvious when someone is physically compromised owing to being blind or deaf or using a wheelchair—it's visible and tangible, and once we observe it, we are more likely to make compassionate accommodations. But when a child melts down in the middle of the mall, screaming and thrashing, it may not be unreasonable that the average layperson leaps to conclusions not unlike those of the radio talk-show host.

Here's where autism cultural competency comes into play. As we've discussed, a grossly overlooked and disregarded nuance of the autistic experience is the acute, overwhelming, and oftentimes painful sensory sensitivities experienced by the vast majority of people with autism.

For example, I filter out nothing and absorb everything around me, just like a sponge. There's very little that escapes my attention, from the distant cries of an uncomfortable infant to the whirring of an overhead ventilation system to the sudden shock of a nearby stranger's cell phone setting off. It can be exhausting to endure. Most neurotypical or average persons *automatically and naturally* discard such superfluous sensory information and are unbothered by it. However, I can appreciate how the child with autism could overreact to a shrill church choir or pipe-organ ballistics; the blaring aircraft intercom that makes you want to jump out of your skin though you must remain restrained in your seat; or the cacophony of voices, clattering cutlery, and swell of food aromas in a neighborhood restaurant.

The obvious response to such sensory sensitivities is to compel someone, through myriad means (like force), to be *less sensitive*—to "snap out of it" and conjoin with the real world.

My reply is to suggest, "What do you think I'm doing every time I step outside my front door?" *The world hurts.* Yet I don't want to be less sensitive than I am. It serves me in my work as a consultant specializing in interpreting autistic hieroglyphics. Whereas neurotypical professionals require hours of data collection, assessments, and observation time, I need ten minutes or less in the presence of the individual with autism to know precisely how to counsel his parents and educators in autism cultural competency: that is, fostering an appreciation for the autistic experience from the *inside out*. Oftentimes I can intuit this information simply from looking at the child's photograph—now *that's* sensitive. My intuition *never* fails me. And I wouldn't want it weaned out of me either. It has value and purpose.

Understanding autism cultural competency includes making compassionate accommodations when and where possible in consideration of someone's sensory sensitivities, much as described in the few previous examples shared here. This requires not only awareness but compromise. I know of parents who insist that their children with autism go to Disney World even though each child clearly protests while there—further stigmatizing others' perceptions of the autistic "brat"—when in fact the behavior is clearly communicating, "I'm in pain and don't want to be here!"

Recall all that I have said to encourage you to focus on prevention instead of intervention; to partner with your child *well in advance* of an activity or an environment in order to equip this very sensitive being with strategies, techniques, and devices to pull it off and get through it as successfully as possible, averting the assaultive irritants that conspire your child's undoing.

And I implore the average onlooker not to jump to hasty and judgmental conclusions but to believe that all of us who experience or are otherwise involved with autism have good reasons for doing what we're doing and that we all are doing the very best we know how to on the spot and in the moment—even the child who outwardly appears to be the product of bad parenting.

PART THREE

Creating Ripple Effects

CHAPTER SIX

Understanding and Using Person-First Perspectives

Recently, at my suggestion, an autism newsletter made a progressive change in its title. The first issue was called *Autism and Developmental Disabilities Today*, but subsequent issues were titled *Autism and Developmental Differences Today*. Does the change from "disabilities" to "differences" seem like a trivial exercise in semantics? It's not if you're the person being labeled—not only as "disabled" but as a "disordered, stricken, and afflicted sufferer." It often appears that those who are normal, or neurotypical, are using their own optimal quality of life as the measuring stick of a successful existence; anyone falling short of that measurement is potentially dehumanized or pitied, or both.

Why does language matter, and what makes it an important point of contention? Language matters because it shapes others' perceptions and makes a statement about the user of insensitive and disrespectful language. Within the last few years alone, witness those high-profile celebrities who have experienced significant backlash for their offensive language; discussion via all media outlets was buzzing over certain persons' very public use of the "N-word," the "F-word," and similar culture- or faith-based slurs. (In 2008, the "R-word" [retard] was repeatedly used for laughs in the Ben Stiller movie *Tropic Thunder,* further condoning *insensitivity.*)

The backlash that prompted the ensuing "rehab" stints and public apologies was spurred by minority and advocacy groups vocalizing their extreme disdain for the egregious indignities visited upon them—because of *language.* Yet when discussing individuals with autism, liberties are frequently taken by defining those very persons in terms of their label(s), limitations, and perceived deficits. Remember, too, that such individuals oftentimes cannot talk or speak reliably; largely for this reason there is at present no single autism self-advocacy group that commands enough attention and respect to hold others publicly accountable for their misuse of language or their stereotypical portrayals of autism.

Making a commitment to refer to individuals with the ASD label (if such reference is necessary at all) in terms of an autism spectrum *difference* instead of an autism spectrum *disorder* is progress, but it is only a beginning. Demonstrating true respect for individuals with autism requires one to be conscious and aware of not only the language being used but also the manner in which one interacts within the context of relationships. It is gracious to employ *person-first language* as a thoughtful demonstration of respect; this means that one verbally values the individual *before* describing that person's diagnosis or difference.

For example, instead of calling someone "an autistic" or saying "autistic child," you would value the person *first* by rightfully stating "child *with* autism." In making the point about person-first language, advocate and mom Kathie Snow asks if you would rather be described as a person with cancer or as *cancerous*. It is the difference between being sensitive and being insensitive, between telling about *who* and telling about *what*. And although it is true that autism is *not* a disease, as is cancer, it is erroneously referred to as a disease and a disorder, immediately implying *dis-order*.

As you learn more about autism and self-advocates, you may understand that persons on the autism spectrum are not particular themselves about person-first language; they may in fact refer to one another with such slang terms as *autistics*, *auties*, and *Aspies*. Additionally, you will frequently hear the same individuals refer to *stims*, *stimmies*, and *stimming* to connote the self-soothing or self-regulating techniques they employ to calm, quell, and maintain (such as twirling a piece of string, or rocking or spinning in place). This does not mean that you should follow suit and abandon using person-first language.

Persons on the autism spectrum enjoy a cultural privilege, a camaraderie that permits them to employ insider slang if they choose to, in the same manner that members of other cultural groups use certain labels in jest or affectionately among themselves but consider it offensive if an outsider uses the same terms.

Why is it respectful to use person-first terminology even though self-advocates refer to one another as auties and Aspies and call self-soothing actions stimming? Responding respectfully with person-first language compels you to be conscious of your words and aware of how you use them. It also means you are far less likely to fail to presume someone's intellect and to talk about them in front of them in ways that are hurtful, embarrassing, and humiliating, especially when they are without a way to defend themselves—just as prominent advocacy groups have in recent times. Unless you have been specifically told differently by an individual with autism, continue to preserve the most respectful approach. You will, in no time, cringe or correct others when you don't hear them using person-first language, and that's a good habit to have.

Should You Use Autism Awareness Cards?

I once made an autism presentation in Los Angeles to a group of exclusively Spanish-speaking parents. They were grateful and gracious, and many made great effort to communicate directly with me in English (I otherwise had translators). When I stood before them and began to speak about presuming intellect and also told them that their children were beautiful and that their children were entitled to the space they occupy, I was stunned by the collective reaction of the audience. People sobbed in relief; grown men, fathers, buried their faces in their hands; and others gave me their children's pictures.

Here was a humble group of gentle people who, as a minority, were already devalued in many ways. Because of language barriers, some may have been perceived as gullible or they may have been left unaware of options where parenting their children was concerned.

They were so appreciative of a positive message that I thought to myself, "My goodness, what have these poor people been told about their children?" I surmised that before this they had felt guilt and shame for parenting a child with autism.

What drives this kind of reaction? Recall that there are several things, in my opinion. First, there is still a very prevalent medical model for how autism is defined. It is listed in the *Diagnostic and Statistical Manual of Mental Disorders*, a fact that immediately sets a precedent for thinking that autism is a mental illness and requires intensive treatment. This is further perpetuated by those clinicians who are not sensitive or compassionate when making a diagnosis or who are unaware of quality resources to which they might direct parents. And as you've just read, the media often stigmatize autism as a tragic affliction to be feared or pitied. You can see how this could create the guilt and shame experienced by so many of my Hispanic friends that day.

There has been a movement within the past ten years or so—promoted by well-intentioned people—of arming moms and dads with wallet-sized *autism awareness* cards. The cards are intended for public distribution in any number of community settings. The purpose is to educate the average person about autism, oftentimes when parents are receiving stares, whispers or snickers, or vocal admonishments. One such card states, "My child is not ill-behaved. My child is ILL. And the disease is AUTISM." Others indicate that tantrums are symptomatic of the autism diagnosis and occur for "no apparent reason," or that the child may "often behave in an unpredictable manner." And then there is the puzzling puzzlement of the ubiquitous, multicolored *puzzle ribbon*, an officially designated symbol designed to represent "the mystery and complexity of autism."

Let's step back and rethink the value of these public awareness materials from your child's perspective. Parents do not arbitrarily disseminate autism cards to strangers on the street in goodwill as part of community outreach; they are handing them out in the middle of the mall, the park, and the line at the amusement park at the height of their child's greatest duress. In essence the cards are *reinforcing* the preconceived notions an unaware layperson may already have about autism—that it's all about extreme, outrageous behaviors that manifest in screaming, crying, hitting, kicking, or destroying property. As the parent of a child with autism, you *know* this does not define your child, and yet you're defining your child precisely this way every time you provide a stranger with such a card, stating in shorthand, *this is autism and this is what it looks like*. You are under no obligation to use any explanatory cards, no matter who is advocating their use. In fact, in my opinion, they are not at all helpful in promoting positive autism awareness.

Instead, consider this: is it your child who is to blame if his sensory sensitivities are at acute odds with the environment and he doesn't have a means of communicating his pain and discomfort? This is not practicing prevention as opposed to intervention, nor is it reflective of the compassionate accommodations required by your child *in advance* of time spent in the offending environment so that he may bear himself with greater tolerance in the situation.

Additionally, you may wish to rethink the autism puzzle ribbon, often used on car magnets, jewelry, mugs, stationery, and other public relations materials. Again, it is all well intentioned but the message this symbol communicates is that autism is some deep, dark mystery so unfathomable in its complexity that it is likened to a grand jigsaw absent the necessary pieces to become whole and complete.

To some, the puzzle ribbon also distinguishes autism in the way that a readily identifiable caste system sets off some of its members, implicating your child as a minority to be pitied. Your puzzle-ribbon bumper magnet may well be conveying that you are one of *those* families, one stricken with autism—and further, God bless you for parenting one of the afflicted. Is there another way, if such identifying measures are necessary at all? Autism awareness is great, if it is done properly. Think carefully on the messages you wish to send the world about how to perceive your child—as having a puzzling malady that precludes her from being a complete human being, or as a budding artist or spelling bee champ or compassionate teacher of people.

The Autism Industry

You are not autistic, your child is. But *you* are the expert on your child. Likewise, your child is the expert on her autistic experience—remember this always! However, autism is also a multibillion dollar industry that is predicated upon perpetuating a culture of fear and guilt that leads parents to think the worst of their children, and compels them to feel they're failing their child if they don't exhaust their savings on medications, therapy, special education, and sensory rooms.

In fact, in 2006, a study authored by Michael Ganz, assistant professor of society, human development, and health at the Harvard School of Public Health, was the first to comprehensively survey and document the costs of supporting someone with autism in the United States. (The study appears in the chapter "The Costs of Autism," in *Understanding Autism: From Basic Neuroscience to Treatment*, edited by Steven O. Moldin and John L.R. Rubenstein and published by CRC Press, 2006). According to the study:

- It could cost about $3.2 million to take care of a person with autism over his or her lifetime.
- This translates into accrued national costs of an estimated $35 billion per year.
- Direct costs—medical costs (physician and outpatient services), prescription medication, and behavioral therapies—are estimated be, on average, more than $29,000 per person per year.
- Direct nonmedical costs—including special education, camps, and child care—are estimated to be than $38,000 annually for those with "lower levels of disability" and to exceed $43,000 for those with "higher levels."
- Indirect costs equal the value of a person's lost productivity resulting from having autism: for example, the difference in potential income between someone with autism and someone without. These costs also capture the value of lost productivity for a person's parents: for example, "loss of income due to reduced work hours or not working altogether."
- Annual indirect costs for persons with autism and their parents are currently estimated to range from about $39,000 to nearly $130,000.

Growing and Learning Naturally

Not only is there no cure for autism, in this author's opinion *there never will be*. Autism has become the new cancer—it is a thriving multibillion dollar industry upon which thousands depend for their livelihood. And it is here to stay in perpetuity. Think about it like this: for how many decades has Jerry Lewis hosted an annual MDA telethon, and are we really any closer to "curing" muscular dystrophy?

Such staggering statistics as those Michael Ganz has summarized inspire grand-scale fundraising in the form of autism walks, marches, bake sales, T-shirt promotions, and related charity events. Do all the well-intentioned people who march or walk for autism in order to "fight," "destroy," "defeat," or "conquer" autism *really* understand what they're doing, for whom they're doing it, and where the money raised for autism charity is being channeled? Is it for autism research or to study how the brain functions? That may be all well and good, but how does that help *your child now*?

Or does the fundraising go for services, such as "behavioral therapy"? Allow me to be clear: *your child does not need therapy for autism!* It is a myth perpetuated by a society that values perfection and seeks to divide those who are "normal" and accepted from those who are "abnormal."

What your child may benefit from are traditional *therapy techniques* embedded naturally within the flow of typical daily routines—techniques that involve you, your child's siblings, grandparents, child-care providers, neighbor kids, and others. Speech therapy, physical therapy, occupational therapy, sensory integration therapy, and more can—and *should*—be woven throughout the course of everyday activities. In this manner, therapy techniques not only become invisible, they're fun! What this requires is that parents intensively *consult with specialized therapists on an as-needed basis* to replicate traditional therapy techniques. (This is how a strong therapist operates anyway—imparting the technique to the client and her caregivers, and then gradually increasing or decreasing the technique applied, prior to fading out). This will require that a therapist makes a home visit (as would occur for early intervention services) or that you and your child make initial office or center visits with the intention of consulting with a therapist to understand the techniques. If you are a working parent or a single parent, then the therapy techniques will need to be imparted to your child's grandparent, babysitter, child-care provider, teacher's aide, gym teacher, music teacher, and any number of other adults in your child's life—but ultimately you as the parent are responsible for ensuring that this therapy occurs naturally within the flow of your child's typical daily routines.

Therapy is not babysitting or respite (those are separate services). You know your child best, and you, as the parent, should be actively involved until *you become the therapy expert!* This is not only the proper response to parenting your child but also the fiscally responsible approach. It will prepare you should funding be cut for traditional autism services, and it will offset (and conceivably dismantle) the purportedly escalating costs of the autism industry. For example, your child with autism may struggle with communicating language but she may also really love music.

A speech therapist may have ideas and strategies that could be combined with music therapy techniques that could then be embedded in playtime or social time activities between your child and her siblings or typical peers (such as singing along with *Sesame Street*'s Elmo in round-robin style, with each child taking a turn at exercising proper enunciation). Your child could also, with an adult, sibling or friend, *sing* the text of a favorite book and point to words or portions of pictures. Or, if your child struggles with feeling connected to his limbs (remember the child who walks tiptoe style), any number of occupational or physical therapy techniques may be used to maximize his feeling of connectedness, but in natural environments such as your home or neighborhood, a child-care facility, or a playground. So, if your child needs to work certain muscle groups through running, tumbling, somersaulting, moving up or down inclines, or using various "crawls" or "animal walks," your other children, his classmates, or neighborhood kids may have a good time doing the same activities *together*. Your child may need to be a giraffe, walking with arms extended up high, more than an elephant, but his relationships with other children will be enriched. Sensory integration techniques involve desensitizing children to certain tactile sensations by compelling them to tolerate certain textures, and one popular intervention is to "brush" a child's skin with a hairbrush. But the same or a similar sensation may be achieved *naturally* by engaging your child with her siblings or cousins to use differently textured craft materials for a family art project; to collaborate with you in combining real (or imaginary) recipe ingredients; to play in water with various utensils or materials, such as sand; to help

happens, parents should intervene immediately and if it happens more than once, *cease doing it!* Your child's "autistic behaviors" aren't behaviors at all—they're communications, communications that something is very wrong and why aren't you coming to my rescue, Mom!

At a recent consultation, I surmised that one four-year-old was experiencing issues of proprioception: that is, he had a sense of being disconnected from his own trunk and limbs in space. As usual under such circumstances, one of my recommendations was that the family should engage the boy and his brother in moving in water (it was at the onset of a hot summer season). Mom's response was to immediately lament the discontinuation of service for aqua-therapy. I thought, "Wait a minute! Who said anything about 'aqua-therapy?'" I was talking about finding a community pool, the YMCA, a plastic wading pool in the backyard—even doing frog kicks in the bathtub. Do you see the difference in how many parents are conditioned to think?

Too many parents are led to believe that more is better. As a result, their children are put through intensive behavioral therapy or one-on-one table-time drills for twenty hours, forty hours, or more, every week. Largely, the purpose is to wean away the "bad" autistic symptoms (such as poor eye contact or hand flapping) and to replace them with more appropriate, socially acceptable mannerisms and responses. The focus becomes quantity over quality.

Given the aforementioned parents-as-therapists position, does this make sense to you? What motivation or incentive does your child have to bond with, interface with, and learn from a *total stranger paid to be in his life*?

Please do not mistake me—I'm not suggesting you *do nothing*. But how you do what you do—the structure, the routine, the relationship, the engaging of passions, and so on—is what makes all the difference. Think on the last time you were lost and stopped to ask a stranger for directions. After you pulled away, you most likely forgot most of the instructions. But you can probably recollect minute details about the day your child was born, your first glimpse of him, and the way he smelled when you nuzzled him close.

This is precisely the manner in which your child will best retain information—by being in a relationship and setting that matter and by having a high-quality, emotionally pleasing interaction, not by being drilled by a stranger void of a personal connection.

Any number of us can recall having been positively influenced, inspired, or motivated by an educator, coach, or instructor who took a personal interest in nurturing our talent or skills and who went above and beyond the call of duty to facilitate our successes gratis. That experience is different from the experience of those children with autism who interact with and relate almost exclusively to adults who are in their lives only because they are paid to be there in order to correct "deficiencies." Further, what of those parents who have relied so heavily upon autism professionals to work with their child? Once their son or daughter turns twenty-one, and is no longer of school age, funding bottoms out and those professional relationships often cease to exist. When professionals are consulted as needed, and therapy techniques are naturally embedded within the flow of everyday, typical activities that take place alongside siblings and peers, learning becomes fun and interesting for your child! (And again, ultimately, it's cost effective too!) Instead of working *on* children with autism, let's work *with* them—and those who love and adore them—to clear up the confusion about autism.

Homogenizing Autism

In my home state, a newly passed bill has been heralded as a triumph for compelling health insurance companies to fund up to $36,000 per year in specified services for families of children with autism under the age of twenty-one. More pointedly, and as directed by the bill, health insurance will now be required to cover applied behavior analysis (ABA), promoted as most efficacious among autism treatment options. ABA is defined in the bill as "the design, implementation and evaluation of environmental modifications, using behavioral stimuli and consequences, to produce significant improvement in human behavior or to prevent the loss of attained skill or function."

Call me a killjoy, but instead of a victory I see the bill as a defeat. It is, in essence, not only an endorsement of one therapy to the exclusion of others (because that therapy is the one covered by insurers), it green-lights the additional, exhaustive expenditure of funds that *no* parent is going to decline if it's there for the taking. But there is a greater issue at the heart of this action.

ABA requires that professionals—degreed, specially trained, and certified in ABA therapy techniques—engage autistic children in intensive treatment activities. Oftentimes these activities are in the guise of play and they usually take form of *drills,* in which the ABA professional repetitively conditions the child to comply with various modes of conduct, activities, and desired responses.

In examples I've observed, the ABA professional, seated across from the child, holds up a flash card of, say, a cow and prompts the child to identify "cow" until he does so correctly and often enough to be considered to have mastered the skill. Negative responses, tripped by "behavioral triggers," are identified and modified in the environment or discouraged in favor of positive reinforcement. The positive response of the successful child may be rewarded with verbal praise, a food item (usually an M&M), favored activity, or toy.

Sounds great, right? The only problem is, as noted, that's not how most persons with autism think, learn, process, and retain information, let alone possess the capability to *transfer* what's learned in ways that are functional and appropriate. And if it sounds similar to what Pavlov did with dogs you're not far off base, though what thrills many parents is *behavioral compliance*—their child has been conditioned to suppress his autistic traits long enough to be less of a "behavior problem" and to outwardly present as "normal." But compliance for the sake of obedience *does not equal success.* It means someone has been conditioned to reply by rote. Further, we've portrayed autism as so complex and complicated, we've disempowered parents from parenting. We've supplanted their ability to develop a relationship with their own children by dictating that a professional, previously a stranger to the child, is solely qualified (and required to be so) to interact with their child for hours on end.

This creates a system of dependency instead of imparting skills, techniques, and strategies to parents that empower them to parent effectively, capably, and competently. One mom was led to reflect that we *all* have to do things we don't like doing in order to rationalize her son's therapy. That may be true, but how many of us as children were required to do something we didn't like every day for hours at a time?

If you want me, as the one with autism, to learn "cow," help me learn it naturally in the context of a mutually respectful, reciprocal relationship that makes it interesting, pleasurable, and intellectually stimulating to learn. If you want me to learn "cow," *show me a cow*. Take me to an open pasture and introduce me to cow; or at the least, let's learn about cow together, parent to child, by reading age-appropriate material, watching video of cows, and creating recipes using the food produced by cows. This is the type of quality interaction that those of us on the autism spectrum record for safekeeping and replay years later as a pleasing recollection.

In contrast, there are precious few, if any, adult self-advocates who joyfully espouse the childhood rigors of systematic programming, and I haven't yet seen any studies that demonstrate how this programming builds esteem and mental wellness into adulthood.

An Alternative Viewpoint

There are innumerable options for supporting persons on the autism spectrum in their efforts to integrate with their bodies, and to tame and refine their reactions to the environment; some are respectful, some are not, and some are simply abuse disguised as treatment.

Parents should use the following queries as a measuring tool:

- Does the treatment presume that my child is intelligent?
- Does it help me further my understanding of parenting my child without system dependency?
- Is my child happy, interested, and making progress?

And finally, a caution: be sure to distinguish the cow from the manure. Your child's future depends upon it. Racheal, one enlightened young mother, summarized her role this way:

> Look at Jay-Jay, look at all the progress he's made. He hasn't gotten this far with medications and therapy; he's gotten this far because I was his friend and I didn't let anyone tell me how to "fix" my son. I've accepted him and embraced his differences with open arms. I've never made him a victim, or a boy who is sick with a crippling disease. He is my son. My three-year-old is brilliant, a genius in many ways! I am honored to be his mother and I am proud to say that I am the mother of a boy with autism!

Because of Racheal's attitude, her son, previously non-speaking, is talking and reading at age three. This temperament will bode well for him in any encounter against those who would wish to compartmentalize him for his "behaviors and deficits." Such warfare too often takes its toll on those who are inherently gentle and exquisitely sensitive as they approach adulthood.

The *Real* Autism Epidemic

As you are probably aware, hardly a day goes by without some reference to autism in the media, be it a newspaper or magazine article, a television feature, or a radio news story. The focus tends to be on the growing number of very young children—two-, three-, and four-year-olds—being diagnosed with great regularity as having autism. Much attention is also being given over to research, causes, and cures; though to date no definitive explanation has been put forth.

As a result of all this continuing, widespread media coverage, we often bandy the term *epidemic* about to describe what's been transpiring with such alarming frequency. *Epidemic* evokes thoughts of a plague or a scourge, which autism most certainly is not. But should the word *epidemic* be applied to autism, the truth is, it has nothing to do with those very young and newly diagnosed toddlers. It has everything to do with autism's forgotten people.

If the word *epidemic* is apt for describing an unaccountable experience that affects people in a widespread manner, it best applies to those adolescents and adults over the age of twenty-one, who have *aged-out*. These are citizens who have grown beyond early intervention eligibility and past the educational curriculum (or life-skills training) of their school years.

This epidemic refers to those with autism who struggle with rejection, who suffer misunderstood relationships because of others' lack of honesty and forthrightness, and who can't land a job because they are perceived as different, quirky, or unemployable. This epidemic pertains to those individuals who have—through no fault of their own—grown up believing all the degrading epithets used to separate "us" from "them." Many of them struggle with addictions to nicotine, alcohol, or marijuana; and they all too often grapple with acute anxiety, posttraumatic stress disorder and debilitating depression. So vicious a descending spiral it may be, that some attempt to end their pain by taking their own lives.

My friend Jarod is one such person who is challenged in discerning the logic of an unyielding society. He shouts and curses his unbearable frustrations. He is a poet, artist, and photographer, and his Web site, with its angry, violent words and imagery, is unsettling, saddening, and deeply disturbing. But it is *necessary* viewing if we are to fully fathom the degree to which *we are creating* a culture that produces Jarods. It is sobering to acknowledge his outpourings—the graphic portraits of his self-inflicted incisions carved into his very flesh—with the understanding that he is but one of *many*.

The escalating epidemic of teens and adults with autism who experience the preceding self-fulfilling prophecy is not a by-product of autism, and is not some twisted birthright curse either. It is, indeed, *entirely avoidable*. Those of us who have the privilege of supporting young children and adolescents on the autism spectrum are learning the inside-out perspective, the requirement to presume intellect, practice preventative measures, and foster self-advocacy. We are conscious of sensory sensitivities, understanding of the genuine need for self-soothing (not stimming) techniques, and envisioning passionate interests (not obsessions) as relationship building blocks.

This is real, this is meaningful; and these kind, compassionate experiences will be retained well into each individual's adulthood, sustenance to counteract a culture of pandemonium. Never underestimate the power you have to forever alter the course of someone's life by demonstrating great sensitivity, pensive patience, and a comprehension of opportunities to simply be the pupil instead of the instructor. You might just save someone from becoming an adult statistic of the real autism epidemic. You might just save a life.

CHAPTER SEVEN

Autism Advocacy and Self-Advocacy

Certain public awareness campaigns have manipulated autism statistics to suggest that every twenty minutes a child is newly diagnosed with autism. Although this may be debatable, one thing is certain: children grow up. Quickly.

Recall that it is currently estimated that there are over 1.5 million autistic Americans, but, as you've just read, that statistic has the potential to expand as the every-twenty-minutes kids blossom toward adulthood. Not only is our nation ill-equipped to serve these young adults, we're divided about the implied financial burden thought to correlate with the perpetual care of such individuals, said to be billions.

If you've come this far with me in this book, you know very well that I'm a strong proponent of the principle *prevention instead of intervention*. Not only should we all wish to educate, support, accept and integrate people with autism fully and as early as possible, we also need to practice preventive measures with family, caregivers, educators, law enforcement officials, and the medical community.

You also know that I'm a strong opponent against attempts to overmedicate, pathologize, and marginalize individuals who have a different way of being in the world. I have devoted my adult life to advocating for children and adults with autism to be treated with respect, and not victimized by abusive ideas and techniques that attempt to homogenize them into others' perceptions of normalcy.

What does this mean?

In the midst of applying a maze of treatments, therapies, medications, and methodologies, it is imperative that we perceive the person with autism as capable and competent. In other words, it is *our* conduct that shapes the future for each child with autism and how he or she perceives his or her place in the world.

In my work as a consultant, I often observe what borders on psychological abuse in the manner in which parents, grandparents, educators, therapists, doctors, and others describe the person with autism *in front of that person!* To some, the child with autism is a patient . . . a subject . . . a "behavior problem" . . . a *thing*.

Imagine having an intellect fully intact, having limited means to communicate such, and enduring constant putdowns and complaints about how difficult you've made *others' lives*—simply by being who you are. It's no wonder that so many people with autism grapple with anxiety, depression, and posttraumatic stress disorder—mental health experiences that society, family, and friends created and could have avoided if only they had changed *their* behavior.

When we don't presume intellect and perceive people with autism as perpetual children, we lower our expectations of them instead of raising the bar and challenging their intellect. Those who are anxious, depressed, or suffering from posttraumatic stress disorder may acquiesce and find complacency in being babied—it's easier and takes less energy. Still others engage in a game of one-upmanship with opposing neurotypicals by regularly creating explosive drama as a divertive amusement—reflecting back what others project. And then there are those whose identity is so closely aligned with an overprotective parent that they become codependent to the point of being unable to make decisions for themselves—their progress is developmentally retarded owing to their inextricable enmeshment in the parent-child relationship.

By not presuming intellect, *we* are creating an autistic culture of learned helplessness. This will make the difference between having forthcoming generations of productive, tax-paying citizens and having citizens who tax the system and are considered "burdensome."

We may use what are considered standard achievements (a job, a place to live, a relationship) as a barometer of success for neurotypicals. In autism, there are many variables that conspire to hinder success on these typical measures, such as acute sensory sensitivities, delays in thought processing and speech articulation, or challenges in motor coordination. These factors make using traditional higher education or viable employment as measures of success inequitable.

Inspired Visions for People with Autism

There have been many famed individuals and creative thinkers who have made significant contributions to our culture *and* who have been rumored to be on the autism spectrum (likely with Asperger's), Thomas Jefferson, Vincent van Gogh, Alfred Hitchcock, Charles Schulz, Dan Ackroyd, and Bill Gates among them. The argument may be that they are all indeed high functioning. But in autism, the perception of high and low functioning is limited only to the physical if we presume the cerebral functioning to be intact.

An understanding that many individuals on the autism spectrum have been creative and productive throughout history requires us to reenvision employment opportunities that will build upon individuals' unique areas of expertise. We know that it's possible to focus upon interesting, detail-oriented work; identify quiet, gentle environments; consider work that is not deadline-specific; and use virtual online employment or self-employment options.

Job opportunities for people with disabilities tend historically toward those no one else wants (or jobs others will only work temporarily). It's degrading to be thought of exclusively in terms of janitorial cleanup when innovative thoughts are begging to burst forth. Helen Keller presented outwardly as among the most severely impaired yet she made a brilliant contribution to the world. Gathering together in support, seeking communication alternatives to speech, and making compassionate accommodations for each individual with autism—regardless of what their level of functioning purports to be—is not only necessary, it's imperative. Creating those kinds of opportunities is what will distinguish progressive, innovative productivity from learned helplessness.

The concept of the dignity of risk should be embedded in each of those opportunities; a chance to make minor mistakes, learn from them, and—with parental guidance—acknowledge good, better, and best choices for future such opportunities. This may give sustenance to your child's esteem and confidence. It may also forge discussions to enhance your relationship with your child as she begins to mature and assume a greater measure of responsibility. But the primary way to *connect* is to build upon your child's most passionate of interests, a concept I've alluded to previously.

The Importance of Passions

What do you enjoy doing in your spare time? Do you like to read books in a certain genre or by a particular author? Do you like to garden, or play a sport outdoors? Perhaps you collect something? Or do you paint, play a musical instrument, or create something using your natural gifts and talents?

You likely engage in such activity because it pleases you, gives you a focal point in which to become absorbed, and allows you to experience satisfaction or pride. Many of us are already aware of our gifts and talents because they define what we do for fun, with whom we spend time, or how we make a living. We may call these pleasurable opportunities passions, areas of special interest, or hobbies.

But wait! How come you can have a hobby, but I, as someone with Asperger's, must have an *obsession*? The difference is *the label*. Personally speaking, I know all too well of the stigma associated with having a so-called obsession, and I've lectured and written about it in many forums. We are all more alike than different—so what's the difference? The difference is the label that creates an "us" and "them" paradigm.

If you spend time watching NASCAR races and collecting memorabilia associated with your favorite driver, you're a collector and enthusiast; if someone with a different way of being does the same thing, it's a maladaptive behavior and an abnormal fixation that needs to be extinguished.

What if we looked beyond labels in favor of recognizing our mutual similarities as simply passionate people? Then the difference makes *no* difference! Each person loves and enjoys NASCAR regardless of his or her way of being, period. Not only that, how does being involved in your most passionate of interests make you feel? Probably *really great* (otherwise it wouldn't be your passion!). You may even associate specific memories of happy events with your passion—if so, you have a history to draw from and stories to tell! Your passion can be an entrée into social dialogue with others (it's called breaking the ice). It may also aid you in learning something new by branching out from your passion into a related but unknown area or topic.

Moreover, shared interests can lead to friendships, or even romantic relationships! When we toss out antiquated and clinical stereotypes and begin *valuing* people's passions, unlimited possibilities await us.

Some common passions of individuals with autism are dinosaurs, animation, history, specific movies, astronomy, trains, insects, and airplanes, to name a few. For the person with autism, passions may be a bridge to enhancing relationships, decoding a mystifying educational curriculum, or developing a *viable vocation*. Such individuals oftentimes possess encyclopedic knowledge pertaining to their special interests or they can lend insights unique to the autistic way of thinking when it comes time to problem-solve.

Identifying Your Child's Passion

For those fortunate to hold dear a passion that is not mislabeled as an "obsession," social acceptance may be acknowledged by virtue of their place in the community and the manner in which they are revered for what it is they have to offer. Regardless of one's differences or idiosyncrasies, our culture *worships talent*. Thus it is important to identify and go with your child's passion(s) as early on in life as possible.

But what of the very young child with autism or the person who does not speak? It is often difficult to discern areas of special interest in these individuals, but that does not mean they are without passions. Finding them, however, may require a keen eye and an attention to detail. In my opinion and in my experience, the following five categories, singularly or in combination, are the most likely areas of passionate interest for very young children or those who are nonverbal.

- Nature
- Animals
- Music
- Family
- Religion or spirituality

Let's examine each area in depth in order to provide detailed aspects that may aid parents and caregivers.

Nature

Having nature as an area of passion manifests in an individual's desire for all things green and aquatic. Trees, flowers, and shrubs, and creeks, streams, and ponds may hold endless fascination. The individual may collect artifacts related to time spent outdoors, such as pinecones, rocks, and small plants. The individual may also seem to have a great respect and appreciation for the time he spends immersed in nature. *This passion could be encouraged through activities of learning about plant life, trees and photosynthesis, pollination, or decomposition; of growing various plants; or of understanding the trajectories of various rivers.*

Animals

Curiously, dogs and cats—household pets—are not necessarily a foremost interest in this category. Oftentimes, farm animals, horses, or wild animals are a focal point. Dogs can be unpredictable and may bark unexpectedly; but others can be loyal companions. Time may be spent interacting with, sleeping with, or grooming and caring for dogs. Attention from an animal may be unsolicited, and some animals (including wild animals) may be drawn to the individual with autism. Reptiles, insects, and fish are included in this category. Be attentive to time spent watching nature programs on television, and poring over photographs in nature magazines. *This passion may be encouraged through learning about animal anatomy or animals indigenous to other countries; understanding animal diet, evolution, and food chains; visiting zoos and habitats; or even studying animal reproduction.*

Music

Remember, music may be likened to lifeblood for countless persons on the autism spectrum. Look for individuals being drawn to specific musical artists or genres of music, or oftentimes, certain lyrics. Those who do not speak may employ musical lyrics in ways that are symbolic and representative of their own voices, as you've learned. This practice may convey thoughts, feelings, and emotions, depending upon when, where, and with whom the particular music is shared. Music may also be employed to calm, quell, and soothe. So parents need to ensure that their child has access to *his* music; it is a misperception to believe that music is not important to persons with autism. As I've suggested, when this has been speculated it has been determined that the individual with autism was being exposed to someone *else's* music or to music played at too high a volume. *This passion may be encouraged through singing and vocalizing; playing a musical instrument; communicating moods and emotions with the aid of music; moving, dancing, or exercising to music; or composing music.*

Family

Notice how the person with autism endeavors to unite her family, particularly a family under duress or enduring marital tension. The individual may be at her finest when family members are gathered together for holidays and reunions, or may celebrate family excursions or vacations. Keeping the family focused on maintaining loving ties appears to be the motivation. Grandparents hold a unique position for having special bonding relationships with the child with autism.

You may notice that the child is attracted to information or photographs of ancestors. It may also be that a child with autism is drawn to the parent who appears distant and detached or who is struggling with addictions or issues of mental wellness. *This passion may be encouraged through maintaining and preserving scrapbooks and photo albums; pursuing family genealogy; researching opportunities for family trips and vacations; or communicating with relatives through e-mail, postal mail, phone calls, and gift exchanges.*

Religion or Spirituality

This passion is most likely to be exhibited in families that are nondenominational or void of any particular religious beliefs. The individual may have profound religious or spiritual understanding, and may demonstrate this through his words or actions. He may insist that the family enact religious rituals, such as prayer before mealtime or at bedtime; or begin attending religious service. An attraction to religious television programs or religious artifacts may be noted. *This passion may be encouraged by supporting a family in identifying its members' spiritual values and determining how the child's activities fit within that framework. Opportunities to reflect upon the ways in which autism has affected or positively influenced the lives of all family members may be relevant. Supporters may also identify positive aspects of family resiliency and perseverance that include the individual with autism.*

Identifying Feelings

When it comes to one aspect of self-expression (and self-advocacy), many parents wonder the same thing: how do

I help my child on the autism spectrum understand and communicate emotions appropriately.

I think the best place to begin is to approach this from an objective perspective instead of a subjective one. In other words, trying to counsel your child about her meltdown incidents in order to obtain specifics might be painful or embarrassing for her as she revisits those episodes (or might trigger further frustration and angst). It's not a bad idea, just one whose time has not yet come until your child is in a place to be more objective and less likely to take the activity so personally; read on to better understand why this is so.

Start by identifying your child's most passionate of interests with reference to what she prefers to watch or play. In a recent consultation, I mentored a professional facing the same issue—determining how to help a child with autism sort through and identify feelings and emotions; instead, the child was experiencing meltdowns resulting from the inability to put words to her experience in the moment of greatest urgency. The eleven-year-old girl in question was fascinated with Barbie dolls and had a number of Barbie DVDs. My idea, in keeping with making the process objective (shifting the attention away from her in a nonthreatening manner) instead of subjective (making her feel shamed or interrogated), was to recommend that the professional carefully review this young girl's favorite Barbie videos with an eye toward selecting specific scenes that portrayed interactions involving clear emotions, such as anger, sadness, elation, and so on.

Once the scenes were identified, the professional made a game of it by reviewing the scenes with the girl—which was pleasing for her—with the intent of gently prompting

her to articulate what was going on between the characters. For instance, if there was a quarrel between Barbie and
Theresa, how would it feel to be Barbie, or what do we sup-
pose Theresa was feeling just then? It's a great way to begin
to deconstruct particular social interactions that can then
be transferred to real life with such questions as, "Does what
happened between Barbie and Theresa remind you of anything that's happened to you?" Not only that, because this
activity builds upon the child's passions, she's engaged, interested, and personally invested in the process.

Once your daughter becomes adept at identifying emotions
and feelings of her favorite characters, you can practice preventive measures such as aiding her to recognize her own feelings
and articulate them before they overwhelm her. Giving her
key phrases to use (maybe even phrases lifted from the videos) or a word or two to convey her emotions should prove
beneficial to all. Even when incidents do occur (and they
likely will, as they do for us all), you may be better poised
to deconstruct what just occurred with her in terms of feelings akin to those of her fictional friends. This is a strong
self-advocacy skill that will be of lifelong value and may be
adapted and applied to any number of children within the
context of their favorite characters.

Another child, a girl with Asperger's, was attracted to
villains as well as Cinderella. If you think about the attraction as a symbolic communication, you'll recall that fairy tale
villains usually possess supernatural powers and have a lot
of control (at least until they're thwarted). And Cinderella
was devalued, degraded, and made to feel like an outsider
in her family—all of which fit (and was confirmed by the

girl's mother) when the child's jealousy was identified and the cause of it was found to be feeling like the least favorite when compared against her half sister, who was the biological daughter of her mom and stepdad.

A Question of Sex

Recently, a group of support staff employed to work with children with autism participated in a discussion that I moderated about sex and individuals on the autism spectrum. Pairing those words together in the same sentence may seem like a typo. Why on earth would anyone want to open up a discussion about people with obvious communication, physical, and social limitations *and* sexuality? Isn't it enough that those individuals, their parents, and caregivers grapple with myriad other obstacles every day? When it comes to people with different ways of being and sex, we rarely want to "go there" in our thinking and our overview of what's needed to support them, especially children.

But, guess what? We *need* to go there if we are to foster self-advocacy! We are *all* sexual beings—yes, even children— and we must prevail in creating an awareness of sexuality within the context of presuming the intellect of our loved ones.

In my discussion with those staff persons, I supported them in deconstructing issues of sexuality in terms of a history lesson. Some of the staff were new to the field or quite young and perhaps unknowing of the lineage of efforts to serve persons with mental retardation and autism. I suggested that instead of immediately discussing today, the group should digress backward in time to fifty years prior. Role-playing a twelve-year-old boy with autism, I asked the group to tell me about myself and my budding sexuality as it would have been seen at that time. Here is a summary of our dialogue:

- *Is autism my diagnosis?* Probably not; my label is likely to be "mentally defective."
- *Where do I live?* Probably not at home but in an institutional setting.
- *Why am I there?* Someone convinced my parents that caregivers were better equipped to raise me.
- *How am I learning about the changes occurring in my adolescent body?* I'm probably not informed about it, period.
- *What happens if I'm caught touching myself?* I'm severely punished and told I'm a dirty, bad boy; perhaps I'm sexually restrained or confined away from others.
- *How do I learn about sexuality?* From rape or mutually consensual sexual encounters with my same-sex institution mates and from sexual encounters with staff.
- *Who is educating me about heterosexual relationships?* No one, the females live in buildings way across campus, for obvious reasons.
- *What if I'm female, and get pregnant from a chance encounter or I'm impregnated by a staff person?* My fetus is aborted and I'm sterilized.

When we fast-forwarded the dialogue to the present day, we considered the propensity for teens with autism to become involved with the juvenile justice system because of sexual issues that oftentimes have arisen from misunderstandings, miscommunications, and an overall lack of adequate information. When we thought about how those teenagers are sometimes treated within an unforgiving system, we realized that not much had changed in fifty years.

One clear and continuing problem is that young children with autism are often so adorable—we want to cuddle them, pick them up, and have them sit on our laps. Those with autism often retain information by association in ways that are very literal and concrete (for example, *draw* a conclusion might be misconstrued literally as making an illustration—and exactly *how* does one draw a conclusion?); but what if I'm now thirty-two *and* I expect to be able to touch others in the same way I've been raised to believe is normal. We've done children with autism a disservice—and created a sexual setup—when we send mixed signals and change the rules without educating the individual, who as a teenager is now reprimanded for inadvertently (or intentionally?) grabbing a caregiver's breast.

In considering those with autism, it is *unpresuming* of intellect to believe that the autism label precludes those who experience it from also experiencing sexual thoughts, urges, and desires. Unfortunately, many parents, professionals, and caregivers prefer the comfort zone of envisioning their loved one as a perpetual child, an innocent unaffected and untouched by sexuality—no matter the person's age, be he twelve or thirty-two. But it is unreasonable, even audacious, to presuppose the authority to regulate the sexual component of others' humanity by suggesting that they "do as I say, not as I do." This portends the notion that sexuality is a privilege held in reserve only for those who appear to be conscious and aware, responsible and superior.

Therefore, children, teens, and adults on the autism spectrum are entitled to information about their bodies, appropriate names of body parts and their function, sexual hygiene, and socially acceptable sexual conduct. Fears and concerns cannot dictate selectivity in determining who can and who cannot receive this information with the same care and caution as would be used with *anyone else* to whom this material is introduced. It's not only fair; it's humanistic.

Nick Pentzell, an adult with autism, advocates acknowledging that awareness of sexuality is commonplace to our humanity, regardless of our way of being:

> So many people tend to ignore or deny the romantic and sexual interests of adults with autism; too many parents want to imagine that it is not important to us or that they can keep us childlike if we are not exposed to movies, magazines, etc., with sexual content. Wake up! Our hormones are functioning neurotypically. But many of us have been excluded from social activities and relationships that would have taught us how to read social cues, be comfortable watching an R-rated movie in public, not pull away from people we like who want to hold our hands, and learn how to kiss or establish intimacy.
>
> I, myself, want to have a romantic partner, hope to experience sex, and would love to get married one day. Not everyone with autism has similar hopes, but I know many who do. The services we receive should be flexible enough to support our relationship choices (e.g., dating, and even living

with someone we love), but many of us are hard-pressed as to how to take a relationship beyond loving friendship, and we can't expect our staff to be put in the position of teaching us. I would like to see an expansion in the interpretation of current specialty services provided in most funding waivers so that relationship and sexuality training can be provided by experts in this field, perhaps in conjunction with sensory integration, movement disturbance, and communication supports. Besides the person on the spectrum, her or his partner (if applicable), staff, and family need to be trained to accommodate intimate needs. Sexuality is an integral part of being human and necessary in seeing oneself as an adult.

Valuing Our Voices

I am often asked by parents of young children on the autism spectrum, "Will my child ever have a job?"

The answer depends upon how the word *job* is defined; but yes, there's no reason to believe that persons with autism shouldn't be gainfully employed—it's just that they'll have some pretty stiff competition. In what industry will they most likely be employable? For one, the one into which they were born: autism.

There are those in the curious business of autism who are profiting, and handsomely so. They are the so-called experts to whom everyone in the autism industry abdicates: celebrity parents and professionals. I'm not suggesting that many of these individuals are not well intended, *but they are not autistic*. They cannot presume to speak with intimacy about the autistic experience. They can only present their objective perspective based upon observation and interaction with individuals who have autism. It is *the latter* who are the true experts; and yet very few are valued as such.

Several years ago, my state government convened an Autism Task Force to investigate the status of autism services and supports in our commonwealth and advise the Department of Public Welfare on action plans to implement and improve the current system structure. Of the approximately 280 individuals who served on this Autism Task Force, there was *no one* with autism invited to participate—all were parents and professionals, the presumed experts. This became most glaringly apparent during task force meetings; that I was appointed to the Autism Task Force as a professional—who has Asperger's Syndrome—was happenstance.

In reaction to the composition of the Autism Task Force, I contacted the state's Secretary of Public Welfare, under whom the task force was established, to discuss ways to ensure that people with autistic experiences would be fully represented and included as self-advocates in all facets of the autism system development. I expressed the critical urgency of having the wisdom and expertise of such individuals carefully considered first and foremost, and the importance of having these individuals as equal partners in this planning process.

During an in-person meeting in the secretary's office, and throughout the interactions I had with the secretary, I stressed the egregious nature of this oversight, to which the secretary conceded. It was inconceivable that the very persons for whom the Autism Task Force had been planning had been excluded from the process! I know of no other consumer group that would tolerate this without serious protest; and, having previously worked for the Department of Public Welfare, I also know that office would have never considered any similar planning process without benefit of a consumer focus group.

Furthermore, that persons with autism had not been invited, from the outset, as equal planning partners in the Autism Task Force perpetuated myths and stereotypes reflecting disbelief of intellectual competence. It risked the interpretation that individuals with autism continue to be oppressed, devalued, abused, and mislabeled as mentally retarded.

Where autism is concerned, I have the luxury and privilege of being verbally articulate whereas many others are mute. In my work, I am well aware of my responsibility as an ambassador of goodwill on behalf of those individuals who are not yet in a position to speak openly and freely in the way that I am. However, I too am treated with tremendous disregard and indifference as people defer to the aforementioned "experts."

If I have diligently made valiant attempts to advocate for all my brothers and sisters with autism to be included— if not employed—and *my* voice goes unheard and disregarded, how is it possible that *anyone* will *ever* listen to those without a voice at all? In my heart I believe that most parents and professionals are well intentioned; and I can fully appreciate their demands, pressures, and conflicting priorities. However, at this time, autism self-advocates sorely need affirmation of a partnership; I'm not speaking of tokenism but a true collaborative allegiance.

Where employment within the expansive autism industry is concerned, there should be *unlimited possibilities* for listening to the wisdom and expertise of those who live the autism experience, allowing them to self-determine how their lives will and should be—and fairly compensating them for their wealth of invaluable knowledge—if they choose to become involved with the autism industry. But unless, and until, we shatter demeaning myths and stereotypes and tear down walls of indifference, the voices of those with autism will continue to be held at bay and silenced by the industry that purports to know best.

Personal Disclosure

Your child has the right to know his autism diagnosis starting at the time the diagnosis is made. What purpose would be served by not revealing it? You're not insulating him or protecting him for the better.

By way of analogy, consider the case of one woman with epilepsy who was never told the facts about her condition; she grew up believing her parents who told her it was all her fault and she could control it if she really wanted to!

At the same time that our society permits withholding such information, it also condones our speaking openly and freely about the most intimate details of another person's physical, mental, behavioral, and educational being. We're most likely to do this with children, the elderly, and people with different ways of being.

Too often, a person's "differences" are discussed at length, on her behalf, and without permission. Such conversations frequently occur in the presence of the individual, be she a child or adult. Usually the person being discussed is without a voice or equal say. Even though caregivers believe they are engaged in altruistic support, a regrettable breach of trust has occurred.

Here is but one example. I was once asked by a school-based training group to copresent on a two-person panel addressing autism and Asperger's. I accepted, and learned that my copanelist would be a professional colleague with whom I had previously worked. A short time later, I received a fax. It was the flyer announcing the panel and the logistics of registration. I assumed it was a draft submitted for my approval, but I then learned it was the final copy and was already in mass distribution.

I was distraught, and here is why: my copresenter was listed by his name, title, and professional affiliation. I was listed simply as "William Stillman, adult with Asperger's Syndrome." Period. End of sentence. Instead of something like "William Stillman, autism author, presenter, and consultant," in one fell swoop I was reduced to "adult with Asperger's Syndrome" and *nothing more.* I was "outed" without my permission or ability to control the dissemination of such confidential information—and I have a voice! In addition, my many years in the field of supporting people with different ways of being was neatly excised; my statewide work as a state government point person for children and adolescents with autism obliterated; and my passion for supporting others' understanding of the autistic experience invalidated.

In a follow-up call to my contact person, I expressed my upset, which had me rattled for days. I thought I was being asked to present because of my expertise, not as a curiosity. I am an educator, not an entertainer. Please allow me to be clear: I am in *no way* uncomfortable or ashamed of who I am, but people will learn about my Asperger's as I *choose* to reveal it, depending upon the circumstances. I certainly want to be known for all the things others find intriguing about me before I'm defined by my "difference." It is a sliver of my sum total as a human being.

The next time you feel entitled or obligated to disclose information about your child with autism, whether he is in your presence or not, please ask yourself:

- Do I have prior permission from my child to do so?
- Is what I'm about to share gentle and respectful?
- Is what I'm about to share private? Is it even necessary that I disclose it?
- Would I be willing to say exactly the same thing about myself in exactly the same forum—or have others say it about me without my prior consent and without a way to defend myself?
- Is there a more discreet manner in which to share the information, such as e-mailing or faxing sensitive information to vocational, educational, medical, or school personnel?

I respectfully request that you reflect upon these words as they pertain to your own feelings and how you'd wish to be perceived by others.

School Advocacy

There's a certain way the air smells on September mornings that I associate with the start of the new school year, and it makes my stomach absolutely flip-flop with queasy anxiety these many years later. It's not because I struggled most with learning (though I don't consider myself intelligent in conventional ways); it's because I felt misunderstood and bullied by teachers and peers. In all fairness, by today's standards, your child's educators may feel overwhelmed, overwrought, and ill-supported by their administration when it comes to understanding students with autism.

I was recently interviewed by the mother of a son with autism for an autism-specific publication. One of her queries asked me to reflect upon how far we've come in meeting the needs of kids with different ways of being. I paused briefly to review my work in this field since 1987 (longer still if you count the couple of years I taught school). I've seen the special ed classes, with those children deemed higher functioning being "mainstreamed" into regular education for a "special," such as art, music, or gym. They were never really included, socially that is—but wasn't that the point, to encourage acceptance from their typical peers?

I told her how I've toured state institutions, rural, self-contained communities to which countless "defective" individuals were sent away—sent away from their families and everything familiar to them. Parents were comforted in believing that the "experts" were better equipped than they to manage (that is, *raise*) their "retarded" sons and daughters from afar and in isolation from their communities.

And I told her how most recently I've conducted consultations at "special schools" for those with autism, from kindergarten age to twenty-one-year-olds. They are immaculate, well-maintained facilities, usually out in the middle of nowhere and staffed by dedicated, well-intentioned people who want to make a difference in the lives of their students.

But I had to answer the interviewer's question honestly. No, we haven't made any progress whatsoever. In fact, the pendulum is dangerously close to swaying backward in time to an era when the segregation observed just within the scope of my professional history was acceptable and condoned.

Special schools are not the answer, but if you build them, children with autism will come; and I am hearing much about funding to erect still further special schools for "special" children (almost exclusively those with autism). I worry that young parents of children newly diagnosed think nothing of supporting such efforts. And I anguish that the multibillion-dollar autism industry is perpetuating the same message that parents of fifty years ago were given: separate is more efficient . . . effective . . . *better*.

It boggles my mind. Not just because all these new brick-and-mortar special schools are technically unlawful according to the Individuals with Disabilities Education Act (IDEA), but because few parents are questioning the wisdom of the social ostracism to which they are contributing.

I'm aware that oftentimes parents feel they have no alternative other than to use a special school, to home school, or to enroll their child in a cyber school. I know that people are weary of battling unyielding school districts. I "get it" that kids with autism are routinely victimized and verbally and physically abused by peers and teachers in ways that should be inconceivable in this day and age. But show me where segregation has been proven to be a *good thing*. Segregated environments are only preparing our young people with autism for *more segregation* after they age-out of the education system, in the form of joblessness, government dependency, and institutional placement in segregated settings. Imagine if it were suggested that we revert back to segregating the races again! It would be outrageous, and yet we are in jeopardy of legitimizing a similar attitude when it comes to individuals with differences.

There is extraordinary danger in ignoring our past. There is also a danger in disbelieving that we are caught up in the midst of a human rights movement every bit as viable and worthy as the advances achieved by women's rights, civil rights, or gay rights activists.

It is not OK that millions of dollars are being funneled into establishing sparkling new, attractively equipped and professionally staffed special schools. It's not OK that we don't hold our local school districts responsible for educating children with autism every time a frustrated parent pulls her kid out of school in pursuit of alternative education. And it is not acceptable that the autism industry continues to complicate and compromise the perspectives of educators so that they feel incompetent and unprepared to educate *children*.

According to Lisa Girion's July 6, 2008, article "In Treating Autism, the Healthcare System Isn't Fully Functional" in the *Los Angeles Times*, the state of California spent $320 million last year for "autism services," up from $50 million a decade earlier (this takes into account the estimated annual costs of $70,000 per child). Nation-wide, the tab is $90 billion annually, a figure expected to double over the next decade. Autism services usually translates to behavioral therapy—which means getting kids with autism to comply by behaving normally, that is, by "reducing inappropriate behavior"—instead of mak-ing compassionate accommodations by understanding that behavior is *communication* and by learning *how* to commu-nicate and interact respectfully.

To be succinct, special schools wouldn't exist if regular schools got it right. *That* should be the goal of all autism edu-cational funding: helping the regular schools to get it right so that segregation—and the prejudice and fear it breeds—is never again an option.

Preparing for Your Child's Individualized Education Plan Meeting

The growing number of children with autism entering our pub-lic education system requires that teachers develop an autism cultural competency in order to have successful classroom experiences. Much has already been written about educating and supporting kids with autism in school settings (including information in my own written works), and I also refer you to books about writing effective *individualized education plans* (IEPs) and collaborating with your child's educators for rele-vant information. But here are some fresh ideas and strategies as well, courtesy of not only myself but a few parent friends.

- Never sign the IEP unless you are 100 percent in agreement with it.

- Take the IEP home and read it over before you sign it. Don't sign under pressure.

- Read the minutes of the IEP meeting; if something you asked for is not in the notes write them down on the IEP and initial them.

- Request a *functional behavior assessment* (if your child's behavior impedes his learning) and implement a *positive behavior intervention plan*. Punishment will not work; it only exacerbates the problem. (One mom allowed the school to keep her son after school for hours as punishment; he was hysterical when she picked him up. She was also encouraged to punish him for crying at school by taking away his privileges at home. She says, "That only enforced his hatred of school and made him feel that I was the enemy too.")

- Tape-record meetings, especially if you get nervous because the other people attending are the "experts" and you are "just" the parent. Trust your parenting instincts. Don't be intimidated by a group of ten or twelve people telling you that they know what is best for your own child.

- Always remember that you are the expert on your child.

- Contact your local autism organization(s) (see the list in the Appendix); they may be able to refer you to a seasoned advocate, at no cost to you, to accompany you to IEP meetings.

- Make all contacts and requests *in writing* in order to create a paper trail to protect your child's rights.

- The IEP should indicate what steps to take in an emergency situation. For example, if your child is upset and starts to run out of the building, what steps will the adults take to ensure his safety without harming him? Laura, a parent, shared her experience: "We didn't have a plan like this and when my son ran from his aide, she grabbed him and held him down (he ended up with fingernail marks on his wrists and bruises on his back). Only when I complained did they set up a plan for a situation like this. The plan should specifically state step-by-step the actions that will be taken to ensure the child's safety."

- The IEP should also include what to do if your child is being bullied at school. A bullying situation is not your child's fault nor should he have to "deal with it." Enforce the school's no-tolerance bullying policy and ensure such measures are included in your child's IEP. For further information on the autistic perspective on peer harassment, avail yourself of Nick Dubin's book titled *Bullying,* and its companion DVD (http://nickdubin.com).

- Insist that adaptations and accommodations be made in order for your child to be educated and included alongside typical peers, who may, in fact, team with your child as peer mentors.

Tips for Creating a Culturally Competent IEP

Crafting an IEP that meets your child's social and educational needs is critical to your child's school success.

Here's one perspective to bear in mind when setting a tone that speaks to advocating your child's perspective.

When I was a little boy, my father would spontaneously thrust his hand toward me with the expectation that I would grab hold and shake it as hard as I could. In retrospect, it was a form of drilling. He said that my handshake felt like a "dead fish." Instead, I was urged to squeeze his hand. Although I complied, I never really understood *why* we were doing this. What didn't get communicated to me then—that I think I comprehend now—is the *unspoken communication* that transpires between the hand-shaker and the hand-shakee that would distinguish a limp, indifferent grip from one that is firm, confident, and manly. Had I been educated about the expected and appropriate social conduct, I would've been better prepared to make my own choice about what I wanted my handshake to convey.

Now consider that at least 80 percent of all kids with autism have an IEP goal to address the requirement for making direct eye contact in conversation. Wouldn't it make more sense (and be respectful in presuming intellect) to first clue the child into the related social mores by educating her about *why* direct eye contact in conversation is expected by most people, and when, where, and with whom it would be most advantageous to endeavor eye contact, and *then* create a goal to hold everyone accountable for this mentoring process?

The goal may, in fact, not be as rigid as compelling direct eye contact but instead may call for *approximating* it (turning in someone's direction, staring at someone's ear lobe, or looking away fleetingly). When you think in pictures and movies as I do, it is terribly difficult to hold that eye gaze in conversation and *listen* at the same time. Can you and the school team compromise in your child's IEP, and make a compassionate accommodation in an instance such as this?

If your child is struggling with portions of the education curriculum, is there the flexibility to use elements of his most passionate interests to demystify what's perplexing? For example, one budding, bug-loving entomologist was having great difficulty relating to a unit on the Civil War until the teacher compromised by allowing her to submit a paper from the perspective of a spider indigenous to Gettysburg.

My own childhood passion for *The Wizard of Oz* could well have been employed to aid me in understanding severe storm systems, the process that would cause a man made of metal to corrode, the physics that would make a hot air balloon rise and fall, or the geography of the area where a certain breed of terrier originated.

Another student grappling with a botany unit felt motivated when he was encouraged to relate it to the pendulous vines in his beloved Super Mario Brothers video game. It may not be realistic for one educator to cater to one child's passions in a roomful of students, but you can enquire about such flexibility; or suggest such collaboration with a classroom aide or with yourself in the evenings, at home. I just heard from one beaming mom whose son's teacher took my advocating passions to heart by allowing him to adjust his math homework to counting tree frogs (his current "thing"). This kind of passion-relating approach may be one strategy to nurture your child's future self-advocacy in aid of understanding and appreciating any variety of topics.

Further, when composing a thoughtful, student-centered IEP, too often overlooked are the feelings and input of the student himself. I recollect attending an IEP meeting for a young man with Asperger's at which everyone seated around the meeting table, including his mother, felt entitled to speak about him in front of him and in ways that were disrespectful and deficit based. When I gently protested, I was told by the school psychologist seated beside me that the young man was accustomed to this because his team openly discussed his "problems" in front of him without his input. This is *not* OK, and having your child's perspective on his school experience is crucial in order to ascertain what's working and what is not.

Questions to Ask Your Child About School

What follows are some questions to ask your child about his education experience. If he does not speak, allow him to indicate "yes" or "no" in a way that he typically does (eye-gaze, pointing, or head-nodding). Affirm that neither he nor his teacher will get in trouble for the honesty of his responses.

1. Do you think your teacher understands autism? (Circle one) YES   NO

2. Do you think your teacher understands your sensory sensitivities? (Circle one) YES   NO

3. Do you think your teacher understands how to help you stay calm? (Circle one) YES   NO

4. Do you think your teacher believes you when you tell the truth? (Circle one) YES   NO

5. Do you think your teacher cares about your special interest or talks to you about it? (Circle one) YES   NO

6. Do you think your teacher gives you enough time to think? (Circle one) YES   NO

7. Do you think your teacher gives you enough time to move? (Circle one) YES   NO

8. Do you think your teacher knows you are smart? (Circle one) YES   NO

9. Is your teacher helping you to learn the things you want to? (Circle one) YES   NO

10. Do you get along OK with your teacher? (Circle one) YES   NO (If NO, can you please explain?)

11. Is there anything else you would like to say?

Setting a Tone for the IEP and Other Plans

Again, I don't intend to continue delving too deeply into school- and IEP-related issues here because it's been written about extensively elsewhere, but I will share some key questions that I think are important to pose to any team convened in support of your child, whether it's an IEP meeting, a behavior plan meeting, a meeting with a therapist, or a meeting to plan for young adulthood.

Asking the team members to respond to these questions should prompt them to keep the focus on your child, shift their mind-set away from an "autistic behavior problem," and drive the collective thinking in ways that foster your advocacy and, eventually, that of your child. (You may also desire to apply this information to your own household.) Start important gatherings by asking the following questions.

- What does everyone like and admire about my child? (If you're met with silence and blank stares, you know you have your work cut out for you!)

- Have my child's passions been identified, and if so, how are they used to bridge gaps in educational understanding, develop social connections with peers, and cultivate meaningful relationships with others?

- How are my child's communication needs being met, and how will consistency be maintained across all learning environments?

- Within the flow of an average day, what works best for my child to maintain focus and be productive?

- Within reasonable parameters, what opportunities does my child have for choice and control?

- Does my child have the means to communicate his need for a break in ways that others understand, and is that communication honored?

- Has a safe, quiet place been identified as temporary respite for my child, a place that is also in keeping with his sensory sensitivities?

- In what other ways are my child's sensory sensitivities being identified and accommodated?

- In what ways are my child's physical health needs (including management of pain and discomfort) being identified and accommodated?

- In what ways are my child's mental health needs (including anxiety) being identified and accommodated?
- Who are my child's foremost safe and trusted allies?

Follow-up recommendations from the discussion may involve your child in communicating what is helpful and what is not, as well as autism awareness education for team members in order to develop cultural competency for the inside-out perspective. Other basic suggestions in response to information gathering may address issues of physical and mental wellness, may focus on preventive measures, and may foster social opportunities by linking your child with peers who can relate to his most passionate of interests.

You may even wish to highlight or otherwise share portions of this book in the spirit of nurturing a heightened sensitivity for your child's way of being, so that misinterpretations, label-limitations, and aspects of clinical pathology will be vanquished.

CHAPTER EIGHT

Future Pathways

There are those who would protest the full inclusion of children with autism in our schools as ineffective, inappropriate, or logistically infeasible. Educators may have been taught and trained to believe that teaching children with autism requires expertise beyond their capacity. Others may be operating from a culture of fear instead of developing a cultural competency for understanding how children with autism think and learn best.

However the bottom line is that inclusion, not segregation, is the right thing to do. And it is doable.

One educator who knows this all too well is Mark Freedman, with the John Adams Middle School in Albuquerque, New Mexico. Though the school has about 85 students with different ways of being in a total student body of 820, Freedman is magnanimous in declaring:

> John Adams Middle School has never met a student who could not be included in general education. In fact, all our students have benefited from inclusive education, like the peer buddy who commented about her new friend Elijah by concluding, "When I came here, I wasn't really used to being around disabled kids. But now I know Elijah, so it's easy to

work with him. He's fun to be around. He has a great person-ality and laughs a lot." Over 99 percent of our students are in "Setting One," which means general education, 80 percent of the day or more. At John Adams, we take a student, figure out what his or her needs are, and try to meet their needs using all the teachers and resources in our school.

As director of the school's special education academy, Mark Freedman further defines the inclusionary process at John Adams Middle School.

Each student with special services has a seven-period schedule, like any other student, and participates in classes with general education students. Each student has an Individualized Education Plan which tailors instruction in the class to his or her needs and goals, a practice made easier by the fact that 75 percent of our school's teachers have dual certifications in general and special education. We have over 70 peer buddies who assist and befriend students who can use extra help. Peer buddies may also include students with spe-cial needs. Each student receiving special education services has a special education sponsor teacher who writes the IEP to include all the tools necessary to help provide communi-cation and support to all teachers and support staff involved with the student with special needs. The sponsor teacher is the advocate for the student and coordinates with other teachers and has their students in at least one class each day.

We also have small classes where teachers can help both general education students and students receiving special ser-vices throughout the school day. Each grade level has a sup-port teacher who collaborates with other teachers who need assistance. Students with significant disabilities also have the continuous support from our paraprofessionals throughout their school day. Our paraprofessionals get the same training, communication, and support as all of our classroom teachers. We have ongoing Least Restrictive Environment education and continuous collaboration with the University of New Mexico in order to keep current and maintain our standards of excellence. This also means that when teachers develop lesson plans, they need to plan for a variety of levels and abilities. Flexibility on a daily basis within each lesson plan is a necessity but also keeps things fresh and exciting for the teachers themselves.

In order to perpetuate the proper and appropriate message of inclusion in our schools, our communities, and the workforce, people with autism require allies who are prepared to disallow clinical pathology in order to promote acceptance. Fortunately, one burgeoning approach that can serve as a viable model for such a movement is already in existence.

Autism Needs a PFLAG

If you think about it in terms of clinical pathology, the history of same-sex acceptance may offer the closest comparable analogy to the present state of autism affairs. In the 1950s and '60s, homosexuality was considered to be a mental illness that was treatable—not a natural variation on the human experience. Treatment of this "perversion" and "psychopathic personality disturbance," as it was known, came in the form of hormone injections, psychopharmacology (drugs), hypnotism, electroshock therapy, and aversive conditioning. Parallels with the manner in which those with autism are *currently* being "treated" may be distinguished for each of these then-acceptable practices (including exorcism as well).

It is easy to see how all traces of an authentic personhood could be eroded and extinguished in those who were isolated, demonized, and absent of loving allies. Not only that, parents of gay children were shamed and stigmatized as well. PFLAG (Parents, Families and Friends of Lesbians and Gays) was formed in 1973. (Perhaps not coincidentally, the following year homosexuality defined as a mental illness was deleted from the *Diagnostic and Statistical Manual of Mental Disorders*, though the "perversion" taboo still lingered.) As homosexuality was then, autism is now often believed to be an "abnormal" condition, and stringent efforts have been devised to remedy this in the form of intensive (read "expensive") methods to deprogram people with autism, erasing their existing humanity and reconstituting them into society's vision of normalcy.

PFLAG is made up of loving allies who are nonjudgmental and unconditionally accepting, as indicated by their vision statement.

> We, the parents, families and friends of lesbian, gay, bisexual and transgender persons, celebrate diversity and envision a society that embraces everyone, including those of diverse sexual orientations and gender identities. Only with respect, dignity and equality for all will we reach our full potential as human beings, individually and collectively. PFLAG welcomes the participation and support of all who share in, and hope to realize this vision.

Can you imagine the backlash that would occur if PFLAG—parents, families, and friends—presupposed the authority to dictate the needs of its constituents? It would be outrageous. And yet identical circumstances are playing out in the autism community. PFLAG does not suggest to speak for established gay self-advocacy organizations, but instead aligns with them in partnership, as an additional resource. PFLAG further defines its mission as an entity that "promotes the health and well-being of gay, lesbian, bisexual and transgender persons, their families and friends through: support, to cope with an adverse society; education, to enlighten an ill-informed public; and advocacy, to end discrimination and to secure equal civil rights."

Insert the word "autism" in the appropriate positions and you'd have precisely what it is I am imploring: a call for compassion and a plea for truce. (One sign of action is that there's an emerging annual "Autistic Pride" day.)

The World Needs Your Child

In June 2008, *Good Morning America* broke new ground by producing a television segment on autism self-advocacy. Not only was it significant for interviewing twenty-year-old Ari Ne'eman, founder of the Autistic Self Advocacy Network, it was the first time on a national news program that a self-advocate on the autism spectrum had been permitted to present a position that called for acceptance and progress instead of curing autism.

The segment was a triumph for those with autism by way of Mr. Ne'eman's eloquent and composed responses, yet in summarizing, *Good Morning America* host Diane Sawyer pondered whether parents' acceptance of their child's disability was merely "a beautiful way of justifying heartbreak." Perhaps the difference lies in individual perceptions.

Autism advocacy, and the concept of *neurodiversity*, is very much in its infancy, and like our fellow human beings with a same-sex orientation, we have a long and uphill challenge to change the minds of those who resist accepting different ways of being or lament the purported misfortune of individuals with autism. But with the gracious support of those parents and professionals who endeavor an autistic equivalent of PFLAG (if only so far in a grassroots mind-set), I'm optimistic that we will eventually draw nearer to a time of universal acceptance and equality. It may be as close as your own backyard through previously established autism support groups; but if not—or if you feel at odds with the position of those previously established groups—start your own group, building upon the philosophies and approaches set forth in this book.

Remember, when it comes to advocating on behalf of your child, everything matters; every thought, every gesture, every deed—and all the emotion conveyed behind it—*matters* in how your child will be received, perceived, and remembered.

I should know, having grown up feeling like an outsider and verbally abused and physically harassed by peers nearly every day for years. I was depressed, anxious, and traumatized, wetting the bed until I was fifteen. By sixteen, I was seriously contemplating suicide. Not only were my teachers indifferent, my parents were oblivious to the obvious, over-looking clear signals that something was terribly wrong.

I never want another child on the autism spectrum to endure what I did, but still they do, for lack of proper under-standing, advocacy, and awareness. Will you choose to talk about "stimming" instead of "self-soothing techniques"? "Obsessions" instead of "passions"? Or "behaviors" instead of "communications"?

The time has come to reclaim your child with autism. Your child with autism matters. He is a human being, not a diagnosis, behavior problem, or second-class citizen. Not only does he require your love and support, he also has great gifts and unique insights to offer with the clarion authenticity of a self-advocate.

Maybe your child doesn't talk or maybe he'll always need help in getting his physical needs met, but that doesn't mean that the space he occupies is without just merit. Believe me, not only does the world need your child in it, the world is counting on him to make a difference.

APPENDIX

Tools and Resources

The three forms at the beginning of this Appendix may prove useful for gathering relevant information to support your child in his or her medication regime (and its effectiveness) as well as for describing alternative measures that may prevent or interpret expressions of pain and discomfort. Following these forms are several lists of resources.

Prescription Medication Questionnaire

Name: _____

Age: _____

Current diagnoses: _____

_____

Allergies (including allergic reactions to medication):

_____

_____

Does the child have any medical history that precludes the prescription of any medication?

_____

_____

List each prescription medication, dosage, and the prescribing doctor:

1. _____

2. _____

3. _____

4. _____

5. _____

6. _____

What is the reason for each prescription?

1. _____

2. _____

3. _____

4. _____

5. _____

6. _____

What is the desired outcome for each prescription, and how long should it be before the desired outcome takes effect?

1. _____

2. _____

3. _____

4. _____

5. _____

6. _____

What are the side effects of each prescription?

1. _____

2. _____

3. _____

4. _____

5. _____

6. _____

Are there any adverse reactions to prescribed medications or interactions between prescribed medications for which monitoring is required?

_____

_____

Is bloodwork or any additional monitoring of prescriptions required?

_____

_____

If bloodwork is required, what is the ideal therapeutic blood level range?

_____

_____

What are the instructions if a prescribed dosage is missed?

_____

_____

Do any of the medications need to be taken with food?

_____

_____

If more than one doctor is prescribing medication, are they consulting one another?

_____

_____

Is there an emergency or after-hours phone number to call?

_____

_____

Are there alternatives that can be recommended (homeopathic remedies, rest, diet, exercise, natural supplements) in substitution of, or concurrent with, prescribed medication that will have a similar effect?

_____

_____

Pain and Discomfort Inventory

(To be completed with your child and those who know your child best)

List the types of physical pain and discomfort historically experienced by your child:

1. _____

   _____

2. _____

   _____

3. _____

   _____

4. _____

   _____

List the ways in which you believe your child communicates each type of pain and discomfort at present time:

1. _____

   _____

2. _____

   _____

3. _____

_____

4. _____

_____

List the ways in which relief is available and accessible to your child for each type of pain and discomfort:

1. _____

_____

2. _____

_____

3. _____

_____

4. _____

_____

Describe the ways in which your child is being educated about pain, including readily understandable ways to express it?

_____

_____

_____

_____

Sensory Sensitivity Inventory

(To be completed with your child and those who know your child best)

Sense	Known Irritants	Sensitivity Communication (How Your Child Reacts to the Irritants)
1. Sight		
2. Hearing		
3. Taste		
4. Touch		
5. Smell		

Organization and Specialist Web Sites

The following list of organization and specialist Web sites is but a sampling of the wide variety of Internet resources pertaining to the autism spectrum.

Asperger Syndrome Education Network (ASPEN). Headquartered in New Jersey, this organization offers education, support, and advocacy. http://www.aspennj.org

Asperger's Association of New England. This association fosters awareness, respect, acceptance, and support for people with Asperger's and their families. http://www.aane.org

Autism Free Zone. A Web site through which parents and professionals can swap autism materials (books, DVDs, equipment) for the cost of shipping. http://www.autismfreezone.com

Autism Living and Working. A Pennsylvania-based group of parents and others who support community living and housing for people with autism. http://www.autismlivingworking.org

Autism National Committee. An organization dedicated to "social justice for all citizens with autism." http://www.autcom.org

Autism Network International. A self-help and advocacy organization run by people with autism for people on the autism spectrum. http://www.ani.ac

Autism One Radio. A service of online radio programming established by parents. http://www.autismone.org/radio

The Autism Perspective (TAP). The Web site for the magazine *The Autism Perspective*. http://www.theautismperspective.org

Autism Services Center. A national autism hotline and Web site. http://www.autismservicescenter.org

Autism Society of America. A grassroots organization for promoting public awareness. http://www.autism-society.org

Autism Spectrum Quarterly. An autism "magajournal" with articles by, for, and about individuals with autism. http://www.ASQuarterly.com

Autism Speaks. An autism resource and information organization. http://www.autismspeaks.org

Autism Talk. An online community with a variety of discussion categories on all aspects of autism. http://www.autismtalk.net

Autism Today. A Web site for the latest news and resources for autism and autism-related issues. http://www.autismtoday.com

Autism/Asperger's Digest Magazine. A publication offering accessible news and articles. http://www.autismdigest.com

Autistic Self Advocacy Network (ASAN). A national self-advocacy network founded by Ari Ne'eman. http://www.autisticadvocacy.org

Autistics.Org. A Web site with resources by and for persons on the autism spectrum, including many links to other self-advocates' Web sites. http://www.autistics.org

Breaking the Barriers. A Web site supported by TASH (an international organization for persons with disabilities and their supporters) that includes vision statements, a call to action, and personal stories. http://www.breaking-the-barriers.org

Brian King. A licensed clinical social worker and Asperger's Syndrome self-advocate, speaker, and consultant. http://web.mac.com/brianrking/Im_An_Aspie/Home.html

Bubel/Aiken Foundation. An organization that supports inclusiveness. http://www.thebubelaikenfoundation.org

Chat Autism. A chat and community forum for those with autism and their families. http://www.chatautism.com

Children Injured by Restraint and Aversives (CIBRA). A support organization for parents whose children have been adversely affected by behavior modification tactics. http://users.1st.net/cibra/index.htm

Dan Marino Foundation. An organization that supports integrated treatment programs. http://www.danmarinofoundation.org

Disability Is Natural. The Web site of Kathie Snow, disability rights activist and parent. http://www.disabilityisnatural.com

Donna Williams. A prominent autism self-advocate and author. http://www.donnawilliams.net

Doug Flutie Jr. Foundation for Autism, Inc. An organization offering financial aid to needy families and funding autism research. http://www.dougflutiejrfoundation.org

Ellen Notbohm. An autism parent and author of *Ten Things Every Child with Autism Wishes You Knew*. http://www.ellennotbohm.com

Facilitated Communication Institute. Housed at Syracuse University, New York, and directed by Douglas Biklen, the institute engages in FC training and research. http://soeweb.syr.edu/thefci

Families for Early Autism Treatment. This organization offers a support network for parents. http://www.feat.org

The Global and Regional Asperger Syndrome Partnership (GRASP). An informational, educational, and advocacy organization operated by persons on the autism spectrum. http://www.grasp.org

The Gray Center. The Web site of special educator and social stories founder Carol Gray. http://www.thegraycenter.org

Liane Holliday Willey. An Asperger's Syndrome self-advocate and author. http://www.aspie.com

Looking Up. A monthly international autism newsletter. http://www.lookingupautism.org

MAAP Services. A Web site offering information and advice on autism, Asperger's Syndrome, and pervasive developmental disorder. http://www.maapservices.org

Morton Ann Gernsbacher's Lab. Gernsbacher's focus is on a belief in competence within respectful, reciprocal relationships; she's also mom to a son on the autism spectrum. http://psych.wisc.edu/lang/intro.html

National Association of Councils on Developmental Disabilities. This is a support organization for state and territorial councils on developmental disabilities. http://www.nacdd.org

National Institutes of Health (NIH) autism site. A Web site of the NIH's National Institute of Neurological Disorders and Stroke (NINDS), offering autism information and links to relevant organizations. http://www.ninds.nih.gov/disorders/autism/autism.htm

National Parent to Parent Network. A support organization for all kinds of parent-to-parent groups that includes connecting parents one-on-one. http://www.P2PUSA.org

Networks for Training and Development. A Pennsylvania-based training and resource organization for caregivers of people with differences, including autism, that supports the use of augmentative and alternative communication methods. http://www.networksfortraining.org

Neurodiversity.com. A comprehensive collection of information "honoring the variety of human wiring" that also includes national news reports on abuses committed against persons with autism. http://www.neurodiversity.com/abuse.html

Nick Dubin. An Asperger's Syndrome speaker and author with a special focus on bullying issues. http://www.nickdubin.com

Online Asperger Syndrome Information and Support (OASIS). A Web site created by parents. http://www.aspergersyndrome.org

Ontario Adult Autism Research and Support Network (OAARSN). A Canadian Web site offering many links to many types of adult autism resources. http://www.ont-autism.uoguelph.ca

Police and Autism. A Web page about autism and law enforcement. http://policeandautism.cjb.net/avoiding.html

Stephen Shore. An Asperger's Syndrome self-advocate, consultant, and author. http://www.autismasperger.net

Spectrum magazine. A bimonthly publication of news and information for the autism community. http://www.spectrumpublications.com

Temple Grandin. Perhaps the best-known autism self-advocate and a best-selling author. http://www.templegrandin.com

Tony Attwood. An acknowledged Asperger's Syndrome authority. http://www.tonyattwood.com.au

Transition Map. A Web site created by Pennsylvania professionals for educators supporting high school students with differences who are transitioning to adult life. http://www.transitionmap.org

Unlocking Autism. A Web site with a listserv to connect parents, teens, and adults with autism and Asperger's. http://www.unlockingautism.org

U.S. Department of Education. This extensive Web site can be searched for information about autism and special education issues. http://www.ed.gov

William Stillman. An Asperger's and autism self-advocate, author, consultant, and presenter. http://www.williamstillman.com

Wright's Law. The Web site of Peter Wright, an expert on special education. http://www.wrightslaw.org

Books for Further Reading

Aston, Maxine. *Aspergers in Love: Couple Relationships and Family Affairs*. London: Jessica Kingsley, 2003.

Berger, Dorita S. *Music Therapy, Sensory Integration and the Autistic Child*. London: Jessica Kingsley, 2002.

Biklen, Douglas. *Autism and the Myth of the Person Alone*. New York: New York University Press, 2005.

Birch, Jen. *Congratulations! It's Asperger Syndrome*. London: Jessica Kingsley, 2003.

Boyd, Brenda. *Parenting a Child with Asperger Syndrome: 200 Tips and Strategies*. London: Jessica Kingsley, 2003.

Brunett, Rhonda. *From Autism to All-Star*. Carol Stream, IL: Specialty, 2004.

Cohen, Shirley. *Targeting Autism*. Berkeley: University of California Press, 1998.

Faherty, Catherine. *Asperger's: What Does It Mean to Me? Structured Teaching Ideas for Home and School*. Arlington, TX: Future Horizons, 2000.

Grandin, Temple. *Thinking in Pictures and Other Reports from My Life with Autism*. New York: Doubleday, 1995.

Gray, Carol. *The New Social Story Book* (illustrated ed.). Arlington, TX: Future Horizons, 2000.

Gray, Carol. *The Original Social Story Book*. Arlington, TX: Future Horizons, 1994.

Greenspan, Stanley I. *Engaging Autism: Helping Children Relate, Communicate and Think with the DIR Floortime Approach*. Cambridge, MA: Da Capo Lifelong Books, 2006.

Hamilton, Lynn M. *Facing Autism: Giving Parents Reasons for Hope and Guidance for Help*. Colorado Springs, CO: Waterbrook Press, 2000.

Hill, David A., and Martha R. Leary. *Movement Disturbance: A Clue to Hidden Competencies in Persons Diagnosed with Autism and Other Developmental Disabilities*. Madison, WI: DRI Press, 1993.

Holliday Willey, Liane. *Asperger Syndrome in the Family*. London: Jessica Kingsley, 2001.

Holliday Willey, Liane. *Pretending to Be Normal: Living with Asperger's Syndrome*. London: Jessica Kingsley, 1999.

Jackson, Luke. *Freaks, Geeks & Asperger Syndrome: A User Guide to Adolescence*. London: Jessica Kingsley, 2002.

Kephart, Beth. *A Slant of Sun: One Child's Courage*. New York: Norton, 1998.

Kern Koegel, Lynn, and Claire LaZebnik. *Overcoming Autism: Finding the Answers, Strategies, and Hope That Can Transform a Child's Life*. New York: Penguin Books, 2005.

Lawson, Wendy. *Build Your Own Life: A Self-Help Guide for Individuals with Asperger's Syndrome*. London: Jessica Kingsley, 2003.

Lewis, Cathleen. *Rex: A Mother, Her Autistic Child, and the Music That Transformed Their Lives*. Nashville: Thomas Nelson, 2008.

Meyer, Roger. *Asperger Syndrome Employment Workbook: An Employment Workbook for Adults with Asperger Syndrome*. London: Jessica Kingsley, 2000.

Moor, Julia. *Playing, Laughing and Learning with Children on the Autism Spectrum: A Practical Resource of Play Ideas for Parents and Carers*. London: Jessica Kingsley, 2002.

Moyes, Rebecca A. *Addressing the Challenging Behavior of Children with High-Functioning Autism/Asperger Syndrome in the Classroom: A Guide for Teachers and Parents*. London: Jessica Kingsley, 2002.

Moyes, Rebecca A. *Incorporating Social Goals in the Classroom: A Guide for Teachers and Parents of Children with High-Functioning Autism and Asperger Syndrome*. London: Jessica Kingsley, 2001.

Notbohm, Ellen. *Ten Things Every Child with Autism Wishes You Knew*. Arlington, TX: Future Horizons, 2005.

Notbohm, Ellen. *Ten Things Your Student with Autism Wishes You Knew*. Arlington, TX: Future Horizons, 2006.

O'Neill, Jasmine Lee. *Through the Eyes of Aliens: A Book About Autistic People*. London: Jessica Kingsley, 1999.

Papolos, Demitri F., and Janice Papolos. *The Bipolar Child: The Definitive and Reassuring Guide to Childhood's Most Misunderstood Disorder*. New York: Broadway Books, 1999.

Pyles, Lise. *Hitchhiking Through Asperger Syndrome: How to Help Your Child When No One Else Will*. London: Jessica Kingsley, 2001.

Sabin, Ellen. *The Autism Acceptance Book: Being a Friend to Someone with Autism*. New York: Watering Can Press, 2006.

Senator, Susan. *Making Peace with Autism: One Family's Story of Struggle, Discovery, and Unexpected Gifts*. Trumpeter Books, 2006.

Shore, Stephen M. *Beyond the Wall: Personal Experiences with Autism and Asperger Syndrome*. Shawnee Mission, KS: Autism Asperger, 2003.

Shore, Stephen M., and Linda G. Rastelli. *Understanding Autism for Dummies*. New York: Hungry Minds/Wiley, 2006.

Sicile-Kira, Chantal, and Temple Grandin. *Autism Spectrum Disorders: The Complete Guide to Understanding Autism, Asperger's Syndrome, Pervasive Developmental Disorder, and Other ASDs*. Perigee/Berkeley, 2004.

Stanford, Ashley. *Asperger Syndrome and Long-Term Relationships*. London: Jessica Kingsley, 2002.

Stillman, William. *The Autism Answer Book: More Than 300 of the Top Questions Parents Ask*. Naperville, IL: Sourcebooks, 2007.

Stillman, William. *Demystifying the Autistic Experience: A Humanistic Introduction for Parents, Caregivers and Educators*. London: Jessica Kingsley, 2002.

Stillman, William. *The Everything Parent's Guide to Children with Asperger's Syndrome: Help, Hope and Guidance*. Avon, MA: Adams, 2005.

Stillman, William. *The Everything Parent's Guide to Children with Bipolar Disorder: Professional, Reassuring Advice to Help You Understand and Cope*. Avon, MA: Adams, 2005.

Winter, Matt. *Asperger's Syndrome: What Teachers Need to Know*. London: Jessica Kingsley, 2003.

Zysk, Veronica, and Ellen Notbohm. *1001 Great Ideas for Teaching and Raising Children with Autism Spectrum Disorders*. Arlington, TX: Future Horizons, 2004.

Recommended Viewing

The following are selected films available for home viewing on DVD. Not all are autism specific, but all address accepting diversity, lessons in compassion, and embracing our collective humanity.

Autism Is a World (2005)

Awakenings (1990)

Being Bullied: Strategies and Solutions for People with Asperger's Syndrome (2006)

A Child Is Waiting (1963)

David's Mother (2004)

Embracing Play: Teaching Your Child with Autism (2006)

I Am Sam (2002)

The Miracle Worker (1962)

Mozart and the Whale (2006)

Mr. Holland's Opus (1996)

The Other Sister (1999)

Refrigerator Mothers (2008)

Riding the Bus with My Sister (2005)

Simon Birch (1999)

Snowcake (2007)

The Wizard of Oz (1939)

ABOUT THE AUTHOR

William Stillman has been dubbed "The Autism Whisperer," by talk-show host Frankie Picasso, for his innate ability to understand and interpret children and adults on the autism spectrum, and Lisa Jo Rudy, About.com's autism moderator, has said, "William Stillman is one of the few who can translate the workings of the autistic mind to the neurotypical community." He is the author of *Demystifying the Autistic Experience: A Humanistic Introduction for Parents, Caregivers and Educators*, which has been highly praised by the autism and self-advocacy communities. His other books include *The Autism Answer Book, The Everything Parent's Guide to Children with Asperger's Syndrome, When Your Child Has Asperger's Syndrome, The Everything Parent's Guide to Children with Bipolar Disorder, Autism and the God Connection*, and *The Soul of Autism*. Stillman also writes a column, "Through the Looking Glass," for the national quarterly publication *The Autism Perspective*, where he is also a regular contributing writer and a member of the advisory board. (He is also the coauthor of several successful books about his lifelong passion, *The Wizard of Oz*.)

Autism and the God Connection, Stillman's study of the profound spiritual, mystical, and metaphysical giftedness of some individuals with autism, has resonated with parents, professionals, and persons with autism internationally, and has received endorsements of praise from best-selling authors Gary Zukav, Carol Bowman, Dean Hamer, and Larry Dossey. In 2007, it was nominated as a finalist for the Publishers Marketing Association's prestigious Benjamin Franklin Award for excellence, and in 2008, Stillman's *The Soul of Autism* was an award-winning finalist for the *USA Book News* National Best Books Awards. Stillman hosts a monthly question-and-answer column, inspired by *Autism and the God Connection*, for *Children of the New Earth* magazine, and he has developed an autism guide for The Thoughtful Christian, a theological training and resource organization. The film rights to *Autism and the God Connection* and *The Soul of Autism* have been optioned for a proposed documentary.

As an adult with Asperger's Syndrome, a mild "cousin" of autism, Stillman has offered a message of reverence and respect that has touched thousands nationally through his acclaimed autism workshops and private consultations throughout the United States. He has a BS degree in education from Millersville University in Pennsylvania and has worked to support people with different ways of being since 1987. He was formerly the Pennsylvania Department of Public Welfare, Office of Mental Retardation's statewide point person for children with intellectual impairment, mental health issues, and autism.

Stillman is founder of the Pennsylvania Autism Self Advocacy Coalition (PASAC), which endeavors to educate and advise state and local governments, law enforcement officers, educators, and the medical community about the autism spectrum from the "inside out." He has served on

Pennsylvania's Autism Task Force and is on several autism advisory boards. He was formerly the coordinator for a Pennsylvania-based meeting group of individuals who use augmentative and alternative communication. He has also been instrumental in guiding and directing implementation of the relationship-based autism training curriculum of Youth Advocate Programs, Inc., setting an innovative standard for the training of mental health workers to support children and adolescents with autism and mental health issues.

In his work to support those who love and care for individuals with autism and Asperger's Syndrome, Stillman sets a tone for our collective understanding of the autistic experience in ways that are unprecedented. Autism should not be defined as an "affliction endured by sufferers" but as a truly unique and individual experience to be respected and appreciated by all. In so doing, Stillman highlights the exquisite sensitivities of our most valuable, wise, and loving "teachers."

William Stillman's Web site is www.williamstillman.com.

INDEX

A

ABA. *See* Applied behavior analysis (ABA)

Abuse, 74; psychological, 136

Accommodations: and hearing, 86; and sight, 85; and smell and taste, 87

Ackroyd, Dan, 137–138

Acting out, 46

Acute anxiety, 104, 132

Acute sensitivities, 81–109; and fostering autism cultural competency, 106–109; and hearing, 85–86; and home, school, and community environments, 90–91; and pain, 96–98; prevention instead of intervention in; psychological concerns related to, 99–106; recommendations for educators concerning, 89–90; and sight, 84–85; and smell and taste, 86–87; and tiptoeing, 93–95; and touch, 87–89

ADD. *See* Attention deficit disorder (ADD)

Addictions, 132

ADHD. *See* Attention deficit/hyperactivity disorder (ADHD)

Advocacy and self-advocacy, autism, 135–168; and identifying feelings, 144–147; and importance of passions, 139–140; inspired visions for, 137–139; and neurodiversity, 173–175; and personal disclosure, 154–156; and preparing child's

individualized education plan (IEP) meeting, 144–147; and question of sex, 147–151; and questions to ask child about school, 165–166; and school advocacy, 157–160; and setting tone for individualized education plan and other plans, 166–168; and valuing voices, 151–154

Age-appropriate life opportunities, offering, 48

Aggressive behaviors, 46, 77, 82, 103

Albuquerque, New Mexico, 169–170

Alcohol, 132

ALS (Lou Gehrig's disease), 15, 70

Alzheimer's disease, 15, 47

Andrew (case), 92, 93

Animals, as area of passion, 142

Antipsychotic medications, 18, 35

Anxiety, 136

Applied behavior analysis (ABA), 127, 128

ASD. *See* Autism spectrum disorders (ASD)

ASD label, 114

Asperger's Syndrome, 2–4, 15, 26, 41–42, 137–138

Attention deficit disorder (ADD), 15, 81–82

Attention deficit/hyperactivity disorder (ADHD), 15, 28, 81–82

Attention-seeking behavior, 96

Attfield, Richard, 70

Augmentative communication, 62–63. *See also* Technology, assistive

Austin (case), 105, 106
Autism, 3, 81; advocacy, 135–168; books about, 191–194; and communication, 47; deconstructing myth of, 20–21; diagnosis of, 11–21; finding hope for, 12–14; future pathways for, 169–175; and healing and acceptance, 23–36; homogenizing, 127–129; and intervention, 33–36; and knowing your own autisms, 14–18; and labels, 27–28; and PFLAG, 171–173; and pity, 28–30; positive transformations brought about by, 32–33; questions about cause of, 30–33; and seeing beyond backroom kids, 18–20; "why me" mentality about, 25–27; worldwide occurrence of, 31
Autism and Developmental Differences Today (newsletter), 113
Autism and Developmental Disabilities Today (newsletter), 113
Autism awareness cards, 116–119
Autism cultural competency, 106–109
Autism industry, 119–120
Autism Is a World (documentary film), 70
Autism services, 6; as behavioral therapy, 160; cost of, 159–160
Autism spectrum disorders (ASD), 2, 3, 26, 42
Autism Task Force, 152, 153
Autistic behaviors, 92, 125, 166
Autistic Self Advocacy Network, 173

B
Backroom kids, 18–20
Baggs, Amanda, 70
Barbie dolls, 145–146
Barney videos, 11
Behavior: aggressive, 46; attention-seeking, 78, 96; as communication, 46, 72–78, 160, 175; self-stimulatory, 60, 89, 175
Behavior intervention plan, positive, 161

Behavior management, 81
Behavioral compliance, 128
Behavioral therapy, 121, 125, 160
Behavioral triggers, 128
Bill (case), 33
Blogs, 24
Books, 191–194
Brad (case), 76, 77
Brain fades, 17–18
Bullying (Dubin), 162
Burke, Jamie, 70

C
California, state of, 159–160
Cell phones, 46–47
Cerebral palsy, 15, 18, 35, 47
Chad (case), 100–103
Child Study Center (New York University), 41–42
Childhood disintegrative disorder, 2
Children Injured by Restraint and Aversives (Web site), 74
China, 31
Cinderella, 146–147
Civil War, 164
Clothing textures, 87–88
Communication: behavior as, 46, 73–78, 92, 160, 175; effective, 55; facilitated, 67–71; offering enhancements and options for, 46–47; reliable, 55; supporting and interpreting child's, 55–80; symbolic, 71–73; universally understandable, 55
Communication, supporting and interpreting, 55–80; and behavior as communication, 73–78; and facilitated communication, 67–71; and pictures, 60–61; and reading, 59–60; and signing, 63–64; and singing, 64–66; and symbolic communication, 71–73; tactics for, 79–80; and technology, 62–63
Compassion, 30, 95
Compassionate accommodations, 48–50
Competence, belief in, 20, 41–43

"Costs of Autism, The" (*Understanding Autism: From Basic Neuroscience to Treatment*), 120
Culture-based slurs, 113–114

D
David (case), 77, 78
Decoding, 81
Deep-pressure sensation, 89
Deficit-based labeling, 27–28, 45
Depression, 132, 136
Diagnosis, defining people by, 43–44
Diagnostic and Statistical Manual of Mental Disorders, 117, 172
Diversity, 52
Down syndrome, 35, 40
Drills, 127–128
Drugs, 35. *See also* Medication
Dubin, Nick, 162
Dyslexia, 15

E
Eating, 72–73
E-mail, 46–47, 63
Emily (client of Mollie), 57, 58
Employment, viable, 51–52
Environmental toxins, 31
Environments, segregated, 158–159
Epidemic, 131
Evelyn (friend), 40
Evolution, 32
Exercise, 95
Eye contact, 84; approximating, 163

F
Facilitated communication (FC), 67–71; technique, 69
Facilitated Communication Institute (Syracuse University), 68
Faith, 24
Faith-based slurs, 113–114
Family, as area of passion, 143–144
FC. *See* Facilitated communication (FC)
Feelings, identifying, 144–147
Foods: allergies to, 87; reactions to, 86

Freedman, Mark, 169–170
Functional behavior assessment, 161

G
Gag reactions, 86
Gage, Toni, 26
Ganz, Michael, 119–121
Gastrointestinal issues, 98
Gates, Bill, 137–138
Genetic predisposition, 31
Gernsbacher, Morton Ann, 43
Gettysburg, Pennsylvania, 164
Girion, Lisa, 159–160
Goldberg Edelson, Meredyth, 43
Good Morning America, 173–174

H
Harvard University, 35; School of Public Health, 119–120
Hitchcock, Alfred, 137–138
Hodgkin's disease, 18
Homosexuality, 171–173
Hope, finding, 12–14

I
IDEA. *See* Individuals with Disabilities Education Act (IDEA)
IEP. *See* Individualized education plan (IEP)
"In Treating Autism, the Healthcare System Isn't Fully Functional" (*Los Angeles Times*), 159–160
Individualized education plan (IEP), 5, 160–162, 170; setting tone for, 166–168; tips for creating culturally competent, 162–165
Individuals with Disabilities Education Act (IDEA), 5, 158
Inside-outside perspective, 81, 108
Insider slang, 115
Instant messaging, 46–47
Intellect, presuming child's, 39–54; and acknowledging that we are all more alike than different, 52; and belief in competence, 41–43; and interpreting behavior as communication, 46; and making

Intellect, presuming child's (*continued*)
  compassionate accommodations,
  48–50; and not defining by
  diagnosis, 43–44; and not talking
  about people in front of them,
  45–46; and offering age-
  appropriate life opportunities,
  48; and offering communication
  enhancements and options, 46–47;
  and respect for personal space and
  touch, 50–51; and seeking viable
  employment for others, 51–52; and
  shattering myths and stereotypes,
  44–45; and ten essential points for
  celebrating/defending your child,
  43–53
Intelligence quotient examinations,
  traditional, 43
Internet, 24, 62
Intervention, prevention *versus*, 49,
  90–93, 135
Investigational medication trials, 34
iPod, 86
IQ scores, 18–19
Ireland, 31

J
Jarod (case), 132
Jefferson, Thomas, 137–138
Jeffrey (case), 74, 75
Job opportunities, 138, 140, 151
John Adams Middle School
  (Albuquerque, New Mexico),
  169–170
Juvenile justice system, 148–149

K
Keller, Helen, 138
Knowledge, as power, 28

L
Labeling, deficit-based, 27–28, 45
Labels, 139–140
Lady and the Tramp (video movie), 20
Language, importance of, 113–114
Learned helplessness, culture of, 137
Least Restrictive Environment
  education, 171

Lego's, 11
Lewis, Jerry, 121
Listservs, 24
Little Golden Books, 20
Los Angeles, California, 116
Los Angeles Times, 159–160
Lou Gehrig's disease (ALS), 15, 70

M
Madonna (popular singer), 65, 66
Manilow, Barry, 17
Marijuana, 132
Mass media, 14
MDA telethon, 121
Medication, 34–35
Meg (case), 78
Meltdowns, 82
Mental wellness, 83
Mercury, 30
Message boards, 24
Moldin, Steven O., 120
Mollie (colleague), 56–58
Mood swings, 103
Muscular dystrophy, 121
Music, 64–66; as area of passion, 143
Mutual of Omaha *Wild Kingdom*, 33, 36
Myths, 44–45, 98, 121

N
NASCAR, 139–140
National Geographic, 60
Nature, as area of passion, 142
Ne'eman, Ari, 173–174
Neurodiversity, 174
Neurodiversity.com, 74
Neurological blips, 52
New Mexico, 169–170
New York University, 41–42
Nicotine, 132
Noncompliance, 82, 87
Nonverbal intelligence, 19
Normal, 20

O
Obsessions, passions *versus*, 52,
  132–33, 139–141, 175
Obsessive-compulsive disorder
  (OCD), 15, 35, 81–82

Optimism, 26
Organizations, 186–190

P
Pain, 83, 96–98
Pain and discomfort inventory,
    183–184
"Papa Don't Preach" (Madonna), 66
Parent to Parent USA (Web site), 24
Parents, Family and Friends of Lesbians
    and Gays (PFLAG), 171–174
Parkinson's disease, 15, 18
Passion-related approach, 164
Passions: identifying child's, 141–147;
    importance of, 139–140; *versus*
    obsessions, 52, 132–133, 139–141,
    175; valuing, 52, 132–133
Pavlov, I., 128
Peer harassment, 162
Pennsylvania Department of Public
    Welfare, 152, 153
Pentzell, Nick, 150–151
Perfectionism, 52
Prescription medication
    questionnaire, 178–182
Personal disclosure, 154–156
Personal space, respect for, 50–51
Person-first language, 45
Person-first perspectives: and
    alternative viewpoint, 129–131;
    and autism industry, 119–120; and
    growing and learning naturally,
    121–124; and homogenizing
    autism, 127–129; and more is
    better, 124–127; and real autism
    epidemic, 131–133; understanding
    and using, 113–133; and using
    autism awareness cards, 116–119
Pervasive developmental disorder not
    otherwise specified, 2, 3
PFLAG. *See* Parents, Family and
    Friends of Lesbians and Gays
    (PFLAG)
Physical restraints, 18
Pictures, 60–61
Pity, 28–30
Posttraumatic stress disorder, 5, 13,
    132, 136–137

Prevention, *versus* intervention, 49,
    90–93, 135
Property destruction, 103
Proprioception, 95
Puzzle ribbon, 117–119

R
Rachael (case), 130–131
Reading, 59–60
Recommended viewing, 195
Religion, as area of passion, 144
Religious belief, 24
Resources, 177–195
Restraints, 74, 77
Retardation, 43
Retarded defectives, 20
Rett's disorder, 2
Rosemary's Baby (film), 11–12
Rubenstein, John L. R., 120
Rubin, Sue, 70

S
Same-sex orientation, 171–174
Sarah (client), 36
Sawyer, Diane, 173–174
School advocacy, 157–160
Schulz, Charles, 137–138
Segregation, 158–159
Self-advocacy, autism, 135–168,
    173–175
Self-expression, 144–145
Self-injury, 103
Self-regulating activities, 89
Self-soothing techniques,
    132–133, 175
Self-stimulatory behavior, 60, 89, 175
Sensitivities, acute. *See* Acute
    sensitivities
Sensory integration disorder, 15
Sensory integration techniques, 123
Sensory sensitivity inventory, 185
Sesame Street, 60, 123
Sex, question of, 147–151
Shore, Stephen, 13
Sign language, 63–64
Singing, 64–66
Snow, Kathie, 114–115
Social ostracism, 158

Social skills, 124
Space, personal, 50–51
Special needs, 1, 4–6, 59, 170
Special schools, 158
Specialist Web sites, 186–190
Speech alternatives, 47, 59
Spirituality, as area of passion, 144
Star-Spangled Banner, 17
Stereotypes, 44–45, 51, 98, 140
Stiller, Ben, 113–114
Stimming. See Self-stimulatory
    behavior
Stimuli, 83
Strawberry Shortcake puzzles, 20
Stroke, 47
Summer (case), 94
Super Mario Brothers video game, 164
Support team, 26–27
Symbolic communication, 71–73
Syracuse University, 68

T
Talent, worship of, 141
Tantrums, 92
Technology, assistive, 62–63
Text messaging, 46–47
Therapy techniques, 121–123
Thimerosal, 30
Tiptoeing, 93–95
Tools and resources, 177–195
Touch: deep-pressure, 88–89;
    protocols, 50; respect for, 50–51;
    unwelcome, 88

Tourette's syndrome, 15, 18, 47
Transformation, agents of, 52
Tropic Thunder (movie),
    113–114

U
*Understanding Autism: From Basic
    Neuroscience to Treatment* (Moldin
    and Rubenstein), 120
United Kingdom, 31
University of New Mexico, 171
Unpredictable noises, 85–86
Unspoken communication, 163
USA Today, 60

V
Vaccination theory, 30, 96
van Gogh, Vincent, 137–138
Veggie Tales (video), 19
Victim mode, 25
Visual stressors, specific, 85
Visual thinkers and learners, 84
Vocation, viable, 140
Vomit reactions, 86

W
Walkman, 86
Wal-Mart, 11
Web sites, 24, 62
Wizard of Oz (Baum), 164
Wojtowicz, Wally, 70–71